C000125261

P&G the Globalization Years: Lessons Learned during Procter
& Gamble's Transformation from an American Exporter to a
Global Marketer

Published by Gatekeeper Press
7853 Gunn Hwy, Suite 209
Tampa, FL 33626
www.GatekeeperPress.com

ISBN (hardcover): 9781662931970
ISBN (paperback): 9781662931987
eISBN: 9781662931994

Table of Contents

Endorsements

Fama Francisco
Chief Executive Officer
P&G Baby, Feminine
and Family Care

"Ed Artzt's oral history is a treasure trove of wisdom, history and truths. He describes the history and the lessons to be derived from it as if it were yesterday. I can't imagine anywhere else where we could find decades of learning condensed in such a thoroughly engaging document. The lessons illuminated here remain incredibly true and relevant to leaders today."

Alex Keith
Chief Executive Officer
P&G Beauty

"Ed Artzt's oral history provides a vividly engaging and powerfully insightful picture of how, over the course of three decades, Artzt led the globalization of P&G. It is laced with numerous concrete and hard-earned lessons from history which leaders will find highly relevant to the opportunities and challenges they face today. I am sharing it with my team as terrific learning and also inspiration."

John Pepper
Retired Chairman
and CEO, P&G

"Ed Artzt's oral history provides concrete and real-time insights into what makes for business success and strong personal leadership today — just as in the past. Ed conveys this learning through stories which are enlivened with vivid detail and lasting meaning. He conveys lessons from P&G's successes and its failures which respond to challenges that leaders in every walk of life continue to face today."

Sundar Raman
Chief Executive Officer
P&G Fabric and
Home Care

"I found Ed Artzt's oral history 'unputdownable'! So many valuable insights and lessons here that are perennially relevant! From entering a new geography, to tailoring product to the market, to the value of staffing the right people on the right jobs, to recruiting, to diversity, to organizational structure and capability building. This could be a business management textbook!"

Forward

by John E. Pepper

Retired Chairman and CEO, The Procter & Gamble Company
Former Chairman, The Walt Disney Company

I am delighted that we have been able to compile Ed Artzt's personal oral history of his career, as well as some of his most important talks. I am confident this book will provide important insights and inspiration to leaders in Procter & Gamble and beyond, today and in the future.

Ed Artzt served as CEO and Chairman of Procter & Gamble from 1990 to 1995. During his 41-year career, Ed worked in every sector of the business. In each of them, he brought strong leadership, strategic insight, remarkable decisiveness and an unrelenting drive to be No. 1.

Ed was the principal architect of P&G's becoming a global business. During his career, P&G's international sales grew from less than 10% to more than half of P&G's worldwide sales. Ed developed entry strategies for important new categories and countries. He oversaw the transformation of U.S. and European brands like Pantene, Always, Pampers and Ariel into global brands. He played a major role in quintupling P&G's reach from one billion to 5 billion consumers.

Ed Artzt served as Chief Executive during a period of unprecedented change in the global environment. Procter & Gamble could not have been served by a stronger leader in this challenging and opportunity-laden era.

Ed foresaw and implemented the bold and often difficult transformations that were required, from restructuring the organization's design, the divestiture of non-strategic businesses, to new acquisitions, opening up new markets and acting on building the diversity of Procter & Gamble's leadership. He addressed these decisions with courage and conviction. He did so in ways that built upon P&G's Purpose, Values and Principles.

In no area was Ed Artzt's influence more significant nor longer felt than his emphasis on recruiting and developing the organization.

Ed's personal oral history provides concrete and real-time insights into what makes for business success and strong personal leadership. He conveys this learning through stories enlivened with vivid detail and lasting meaning. The speeches and portions of speeches included here capture the breadth and depth of Ed Artzt's contributions. They convey lessons from P&G's successes and failures, and they outline challenges the Company faced then and continues to face today.

I had the benefit and privilege of working for Ed Artzt for almost half of my 40-year career. I personally experienced his unrelenting commitment to the development of the individual.

I can recall this from my very first months in the Company. Ed was the Brand Promotion Manager in my group. I was a Brand Assistant, three levels below him. I remember him spending literally hours with me in his office, one on one, talking about the principles of the business, what makes for a good copy strategy, how to gain a competitive edge and much more. Those conversations formed the basis of my business education at P&G. They guided my business decisions throughout my career. They demonstrated his concern for my development.

Ed's focus on training and development of P&G people was unrelenting. He brought recruiting to a whole new level. He introduced P&G College. He spent time on college campuses.

As he advised students in his powerful *How to Become a Winning Manager* talk, "Work for people who care about your progress — not just your performance, but your progress, your growth. There is a big difference."

Above all, Ed was committed to winning. He told shareholders in 1994, "We want to be the best at everything we do, because we know that's what it takes to drive our brands to market leadership." He rolled up his sleeves to lead and do whatever was necessary to achieve that goal. He called things as he saw them — always trying to do the right thing.

As I reflect on Ed Artzt's legacy, I return to his deep respect for P&G people and for the important role that each of us can play as individuals. "This is not a company of ordinary individuals," Ed said in a 1993 speech. "It's an organization of high-energy, creative, articulate people who like to set higher standards for themselves than anyone else can set for them."

That's true — and especially so for Ed Artzt.

John E. Pepper

Section

01

P&G
The Globalization Years

An Oral History by Former P&G Chairman and CEO Ed Artzt

Note: This interview with Ed Artzt was conducted by John Pepper, former P&G CEO, Shane Meeker, P&G Corporate Historian and Rob Garver, author and journalist.

Lessons Learned During Procter & Gamble's Transformation From an American Exporter to a Global Marketer

Background: The question was raised as to why P&G switched from a family partnership to a public company without any member of the two families in the management.

Ed Artzt	William Cooper Procter was the last family member to run the Company. He was President for 23 years, and by the time he retired in 1930, there was hardly anybody in the family that had worked as a manager at P&G. It was all pretty much cleaned out. William Cooper Procter had four sisters. He was married, but childless, and there were no male heirs, other than a few distant cousins that did not work for P&G.
John Pepper	It was his decision not to hire any members of the family?
Ed Artzt	Yes. Harley Procter, who was Cooper's cousin, did a good job as Sales and Advertising Manager. Harley was 10 years older than Cooper, and he was anxious to retire early and move to upstate New York where he lived in the summer. So, there were no natural successors or future employees who were members of the family.

The decision to choose a non-family member to run P&G was actually a long time in the making. The Gamble families had already drifted away from active involvement in the business and were largely living an aristocratic life in Cincinnati and in the Hamptons. They had already ceded leadership of P&G by the time that William Cooper Procter became President and CEO.

The Gambles had become very active in the Cincinnati community and had separately established a vigorous social life in the Hamptons. P&G had a tradition of starting its future family members in the factories, and this kind of devotion to factory experience had lost its appeal to successive generations of family members.

Meanwhile, Cooper Procter was a guy who was visionary enough to see the need to build up an organization of non-family members. His choice of a successor, RR Deupree, seemed to be the last person in the world that they would ever choose as the next Chief of the Company. Deupree had left school in Covington, Kentucky, at the age of 16 to work for the Cincinnati Street Railway. He joined P&G at the age of twenty two and wound up being President for 18 years and Chairman for another 11 years after that. He was brilliant.

RR Deupree was a very strong and successful leader of the Company. But, he was stubbornly opposed to expanding the Company's investment in Europe during the years between the

William Cooper
Procter

two world wars. He believed that one world war was enough and he didn't want the Company to get exposed to another situation where it would lose employees and assets to a violent war.

The years between World War I and World War II were critical to the development of P&G, as we know it today, because it marked the transition from soap to synthetic laundry detergents and from a U.S.-based company to an international company with an important foothold in Europe. The hierarchy at that time was Deupree, Chairman and CEO, Neil McElroy, President, Jake Lingle, Executive VP in charge of International and Morton Woodward, Vice President of Manufacturing of International markets reporting to Jake Lingle.

Neil
McElroy

WWII had left our competitors in Europe in virtual ashes.
Unilever and Henkle's major factories had been destroyed.
P&G had introduced Dreft in the Benelux in 1933, but it was
a light-duty product targeted to new mothers and baby clothes
because it did not perform very well on dirty clothes in hard water.
However, beginning in 1946, Tide entered test markets in the
United States, and the race was on. It took three years to complete
the Tide expansion. Meanwhile, Unilever was gaining an early
foothold in synthetic detergents in Western Europe, and Henkel
was doing the same in Germany.

RR Deupree had been very reluctant for P&G to reinvest in Europe prior to WWII. He was concerned about P&G suffering the
kind of losses of people and assets that our competitors had lost if

we made major investments in Europe and a third war followed. Deupree's concerns were not shared by McElroy and Lingle.

The biggest concern was that Unilever had already started early production of synthetic detergents in Europe as they embarked on a strategy of trying to beat Procter into Europe while P&G was focused on Tide in the U.S.

At some point in the late 1940s or early '50s, Neil McElroy charged Jake Lingle with the responsibility for finding an existing factory with a synthetic detergent tower that P&G could convert to Tide in one of the major countries in Europe. Lingle had negotiated for the purchase of the Marseille plant in France but was unable to consummate the deal until Deupree agreed. As Jake Lingle told the story, it was McElroy who took matters into his own hands and told Jake to go ahead and buy

Jake
Lingle

the Marseille factory and, "I will handle Mr. Deupree," and that is exactly what happened.

Another important player in the detergent business was Morton Woodward. He had been charged by his top management bosses to carefully control any allocations of U.S. Tide production capacity that might be diverted to the International Division.

John, wasn't your wife, Francie, related to Woodward?

John Pepper   Sure, he is Francie's great uncle.

Ed Artzt   Anyway, Woodward's approach was effective but devastatingly inflexible. It consisted of two rules: 1) No U.S. Tide could be diverted to International if it slowed Tide expansion in the United

Morton
Woodward

"We believe in confining our product failures to test markets rather than allowing ourselves to blow national expansion of the wrong product on a new brand."

— Ed Harness, Former P&G Chairman & CEO

States. 2) Only the U.S. Tide product could be produced for the International Division until U.S. expansion was completed.

These rules were put into place despite the fact that the International Division was pleading for at least test quantities of Tide product that would be modified to better perform under European laundering conditions. But, no dice.

U.S. Tide was designed to perform in 16 gallons of water in agitator washing machines. Most European machines were drum machines that cleaned in about 8 gallons of water. U.S. Tide over-sudsed in drum machines, causing consumers to cut back on product dosage and as a result experience poorer performance.

European P&G management feared that Tide would fail, but when U.S. Tide became available, they charged ahead anyway. Tide was a dud everywhere but Saudi Arabia, where hand washing was the main usage for laundry detergent.

Howard
Morgens

Latin America was a different story. When Colgate saw that
P&G was shipping only U.S. Tide into new foreign markets, they
increased the surfactant level of their laundry brands and out
sudsed Tide for hand washing, the prevalent method of cleaning
clothes in countries with low washing machine penetration.
Thus, Tide flopped in Mexico for not making enough suds in a
tub or a bucket.

I am reminded that Ed Harness used to say that we believe in
confining our product failures to test markets rather than allow-
ing ourselves to blow national expansion of the wrong product
on a new brand. Our failure to get the right Tide product into
international markets was a hugely costly mistake. Our entry into
the laundry category in Europe, for example, was delayed for
more than a decade until Ariel was launched in several different

product forms in the 1960s, starting with the UK in 1967.

Again, in my judgment, there should have been pushback by the International leadership to convince the Company to produce test market quantities of the European Tide formula early on. Ditto for Mexican Tide. Finally, I strongly suspect that there was a touch of unwarranted overoptimism within the U.S. management – a mistaken belief that what works well with the U.S. consumer should work equally well in international markets. Unfortunately,

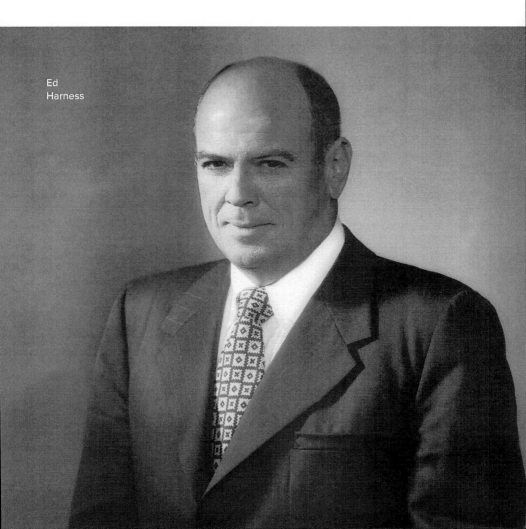

Ed
Harness

Bill
Gurganus

we had to learn that painful lesson more than once.

John Pepper   We went through the same thing, didn't we, in Japan, when
               we introduced products that weren't suitable for Japan?

Ed Artzt   True, but P&G's entry into Japan was also impacted by unprec-
            edented changes at the top of the Company. The decision to
            enter Japan in 1973, by acquiring a virtually bankrupt detergent
            company, was made by Howard Morgens after much internal de-
            bate. The prevailing argument in favor of the investment was that
            we needed to learn how to compete with Japanese companies in
            their backyards before they invaded ours. Good thought, but bad
            timing for P&G.

            In the midst of the Japan discussion with the Board, Neil McElroy, Chairman of the Board, died tragically of pancreatic cancer in December 1972, setting off a chain reaction of changes at the top of the Company that undoubtedly diverted attention away from the huge challenges Japan represented.

1. The most critical of those events came from Bill Gurganus, head of P&G's International Business.

2. To Mr. Morgen's surprise, Bill refused to accept the top responsibility for Japan. Bill was clearly the most successful and experienced international leader in the Company. He had run Germany and managed the development of Ariel, but he had strongly argued against entering Japan. He felt that we did not have the products and people to enter the toughest international market in the world, and that we needed a great deal more due diligence before taking on such a risky project. Bill also hated to fly, and he was firmly opposed to the idea of the 14-hour overseas flights back and forth to Japan.

Bill Gurganus continued to run the International business except Japan and the Philippines. Brad Butler, formerly Sales Vice President of the Company and the Company's Chief Staff Officer, was then given responsibility for Japan. Brad had served in the U.S. Military Intelligence divisions during WWII and could speak some Japanese. He also understood Japanese culture, but Brad had not run any of P&G's foreign business requiring product invention.

The biggest discontinuity of all, of course, was the 1974 retirement of Howard Morgens and the election of Ed Harness as CEO of the Company. This happened less than a year after the acquisition of our Japanese subsidiary. Ed Harness had obtained the Board's approval to appoint Brad Butler as Vice Chairman, with responsibility for all of the Company's staff operations, thereby relegating Brad's responsibility for Japan to much less

Brad
Butler

than a full-time job. Brad felt that he could handle Japan because he believed we could succeed in Japan with U.S. products, including All Temperature Cheer and U.S. Pampers. And that mistake proved to be every bit as devastating as the earlier failed effort to sell U.S. Tide in Europe and Latin America.

Ed Harness, of course, was fully capable of making the right decisions for Japan, but Ed had a huge new job to undertake. So he had to depend on Brad Butler and the people under Brad to exercise the right judgment while Ed focused his full attention on running the Procter & Gamble Company. The people under Brad Butler included Ed Shutt as Division Manager, Asia. Shutt had worked in Clorox and also had no international experience. Shutt left the Company in 1977, one year after overseeing the introduction of All Temperature Cheer in a country where consumers washed their clothes by transferring warm water from their bath to their washing machines; there was no choice of temperatures as in the United States.

"Remember, our early experience overseas was largely gained with the export of U.S. brands."

I was not a candidate to run Japan because in 1976, I was only in the second year of my five-year tour in Europe. I returned to the U.S. in 1980 when John Smale became Chief Executive. Japan at that point was $300 million in the red, and the Board was urging us to fix things quickly or write it off and pull out. John and I weren't about to quit on Japan once we discovered how many fixable mistakes had been made. My involvement in Japan was delayed until 1982.

I've never completely understood the dichotomy between the Company's determination to expand the business internationally and the Company's unwillingness to do so with products tailored to local conditions, habits and practices. It may be that until Tide came along in the 1940s, the need didn't exist in our industry. Synthetic detergents were the game-changer.

Remember, our early experience overseas was largely gained with exports of U.S. brands. Early on, U.S. brands were sold worldwide by an export office in New York. The first export organization was an arm of the Sales Department, and its customers were small outlets servicing U.S. citizens living abroad and tourists. Volumes were small. Prices were high. Overheads were minuscule and, considering there was no advertising support behind these

"We are reminded that history isn't made in a vacuum. Good things happen. Bad things happen, and unforeseen circumstances intervene. The result can be a win for the Company that makes the fewest mistakes."

Samih Sherif

exports, profitability was decent, albeit inconsequential in total. Nevertheless, it gave some support to the notion that American products could be marketed successfully overseas.

Later, as the export business grew, the organization was moved to London under Jake Lingle, and it subsequently moved to Geneva and added the "Special Operations" function, under Samih Sherif. The Special Operations Group was our first venture into smaller countries with local manufacturing operated under partnerships or joint ventures — countries like Greece, Lebanon, Saudi Arabia and Egypt. These countries needed product development support for their manufacturing operations, and we were able to adapt their detergent formulas to local habits and laundry equipment, utilizing the same group that was supporting production in Marseille, Belgium and the UK.

At the same time that the Company was expanding its export operation overseas, the Company had separately gained important footholds with local brands in the UK, Mexico, the Benelux and the Philippines, dating back as far as 1930 in the UK and 1935 in the Philippines.

Both Neil McElroy and Jake Lingle had separately managed our UK subsidiary pre WWII. So how did they underestimate the need for product tailoring overseas? They, and others under them, were brilliant P&G leaders and excellent marketers, so I can only conclude that our post war mistakes traced to the fact that the need for tailoring didn't exist until our first game-changing technology came along with the replacement of heavy-duty fat soaps with synthetic detergents.

Ivory Soap is worth a mention here. To my knowledge, we never tried to launch Ivory Soap in Europe, for example, because Europe had mostly hard water, and Ivory bar soap had relatively poor acceptance in hard water markets in the U.S. Since the Company had a firm policy of not tampering with the Ivory product formula, it never really qualified for international expansion, and thus contributed very little to our foreign experience base.

Looking back, we are reminded that history isn't made in a vacuum. Good things happen. Bad things happen, and unforeseen circumstances intervene. The net result can be a win for the company that makes the fewest mistakes.

Had I been running the Company in the 1940s, I probably would have made the same decision regarding U.S. Tide expansion priority. Laundry products were our core business and getting Tide into U.S. markets first was essential to our future leadership of that category. So I believe that P&G made the right call on Tide.

However, I believe we should have pushed harder to obtain

production capacity capable of giving us early quantities of foreign Tide formulas in order to make certain that we had the right products for success overseas. Not doing that was a mistake that cost us several years in the detergent race in Europe. But charging into Europe with the U.S. Tide product was a far bigger mistake because it killed the Tide brand in most foreign markets it entered.

The differences between washing machines in Germany and the United States, for example, were so great that it is hard to imagine that knowledgeable people believed that the U.S. Tide product would gain good acceptance by consumers outside the United States. U.S. washing machines received their water from the hot water faucet, and the average water temperature was about 104 degrees Fahrenheit. German machines, on the other hand, heated the wash water within the machines, enabling consumers to prewash at low temperatures and boil wash at very high temperatures, all in the same machine.

Also, U.S. machines were mostly top loaders with water capacity of about 16 gallons, while most Europeans machines were front loaders with water capacity of eight gallons. These required significant differences in product formulation, especially to deal with suds sensitivity. After the war, Europeans laundered their clothes less frequently than American consumers, and thus soiling conditions required more robust cleaning products than U.S. Tide.

Shane Meeker

So, one of the primary reasons why Tide didn't work was the appliance and consumer habits were just so different between the two regions.

Ed Artzt

Correct. Think of it this way: We had invented a new laundry detergent that outperformed existing heavy-duty fat soaps in top loading washers and also for hand washing in tubs and buckets in developing markets. It was very sudsy, and women used suds as the guide to dosage in their machines. In fact, the original Tide package carried the words, "Oceans of Suds." Tide advertising in the 50's celebrated the promise that "Tide suds keep on working after other suds have quit." Tide had been designed that way.

So we put a product into Europe that keeps on working after suds have quit. We instructed consumers to use it in a machine that doesn't want suds and doesn't work well with too many suds. People were underusing the product because it made too many suds. They thought the product was unsafe for their machines, and it failed. It didn't just fall short, it failed.

John Pepper

We made the same mistake with Japan. We also made the same mistake years later in Morocco where we

MINIMUM WEIGHT 18 OZ. THE BIOLOGICAL WASHING MIRACLE

ARIEL

DIGESTS DIRT AND STAINS THAT ORDINARY POWDERS LEAVE BEHIND

thought we would do something really smart and reduce suds, and they wanted more suds in Morocco. We're smart people. Why do you think we fail to learn from history in the way we have?

Ed Artzt   I really don't know. It could have been a form of arrogance, which tends to afflict very successful companies. This type of arrogance comes in at least two flavors, both dangerous. One happens when management says, "We're aware of the shortcomings, but we can overcome them with our successful U.S. products and approaches." This one killed Tide and undoubtedly nearly buried us in Japan. The other flavor, equally deadly, says, "We're aware of the shortcomings, and they cannot be overcome." This one brought us Luvs, instead of shaped Pampers, and helped Kimberly-Clark achieve leadership in the diaper category, as Pampers struggled with less than the best P&G product.

"Ariel was one of the Company's first big successes at tailoring products to local conditions in foreign countries."

We were fortunate the Company got a second chance at revolutionizing the detergent market in foreign countries. R&D had successfully incorporated enzymes in a conventional European HD detergent, which led to the 1967 introduction of Ariel in multiple foreign markets. Europe launched two iterations. In Germany, Ariel started as a concentrated pre-wash product which was used together with a through-the-wash detergent, usually Henkel's Persil. Italy followed Germany, while the rest of Europe patterned Ariel after the range of through-the-wash detergents designed for European top loading machines. This was one of the Company's first big successes at tailoring products to local conditions in foreign countries.

I spent three years in the paper division from 1965 to 1968. Not very long, but they were incredibly eventful times. P&G had acquired the Charmin Company in 1957 in the belief that we were on the brink of revolutionizing tissue making, with a process called TAD, or blow-through air drying. This gave our tissue products a very highly significant advantage over our competition in product softness and cost per use because it required less pulp to make each comparable sheet of tissue. Inside P&G, the product was called CPF.

P&G's entire disposable venture had more proprietary technology on the drawing board than most companies invent in their lifetime. In addition to the TAD process for tissue products, there was the knob to knob converting technology for high-speed bonding of two-ply paper towels (Bounty) — a real breakthrough in absorbency.

And of course, there were several process inventions that gave us Pampers, including high-speed bonding of top and bottom sheets plus converting line speeds of over 400 diaper pads per minute. In many ways, the inventions that underpinned our entry into disposables personified the Company's greatest R&D strength over the decades — the field of Process Development, or the art of putting things together in novel ways that result in superior consumer products. Think of Ivory Soap, Crisco and Tower blown laundry detergents. The genius that produced Pampers, Bounty, Pringles and Swiffer was no accident. It was inextricably linked by the incredibly gifted teams of engineers, R&D scientists and manufacturing process specialists who made difficult things work.

Unfortunately, in the case of disposables, they didn't always work quickly, easily or efficiently. In fact, the situation was such a mess that Howard Morgens moved Ed Harness from soap to paper, and gave Ed a virtual blank check to get the people and resources he needed to turn things around. Ed was Howard's eventual successor as the head of the Company, so steeping him in this capital-intensive paper startup was a very wise move by Morgens.

Ed Harness quickly proceeded to cherry-pick the Soap Division in order to hand select the talent he wanted to join him in Paper.

The key players and their responsibilities were Chuck Fullgraf, General Manager Paper, Harry Tecklenburg, Manager R&D and Process Development, Jim Edwards, Manager of Manufacturing, Fred Wells, Manager of Process Development. And I was Manager of Advertising. Fred was one of the inventors of CPF and perhaps the best Process Development engineer in the Company. Chuck Fullgraf had extensive manufacturing experience, including the highly classified responsibility for managing the Milan Arsenal during WWII, which produced munitions for the war.

The main problem that had to be solved was the difficulty of manufacturing scale-up. There were no commercially available paper machines that could make CPF paper. All the paper machines at Charmin's Green Bay plant were only able to make

"The inventions that underpinned our entry into disposables personified the Company's greatest R&D strength over the decades — the field of process development, or the art of putting things together in novel ways that result in superior consumer products."

conventional tissue, and they had all been upgraded to give us blind test wins over our leading competition. But it wasn't enough; Puffs and White Cloud were struggling badly in test markets, and Charmin was not growing in established markets and was nowhere near ready for national expansion. Clearly, we had to have CPF to succeed in the toilet and facial tissue categories in the paper business. Bounty was successful and expanding because of its converting invention, but blind tests showed a major preference for its CPF version.

The only CPF paper capacity pre-Ed Harness was the prototype papermaking machine that could support blind testing and small area ship testing. The CPF test results had been terrific. The consumers loved the product, but scaling the process up to full factory production was like scaling up a row boat to become a battleship. The prototype was designed to produce a sheet of toilet paper 12 feet wide at a rate of 3,000 feet a minute, but we had to invest $30 million in a gigantic new machine in order to find out if we could deliver its designed production rate.

What was even more daunting was the fact that the Company had simultaneously invested over a $100 million in a new tissue plant in Mehoopany, PA, in order to be closer to an abundant supply of short fiber trees, an essential ingredient in CPF tissue. The first scaled-up CPF paper machine was located in Mehoopany. Quite a crapshoot now that I think about it.

I remember several times when Chuck Fullgraf and I joined Ed Harness in his office at days end to get the daily report on the number one CPF paper machine from our plant manager at Mehoopany. For months, the reports were grim. Every time the machine rate was elevated to anything close to 3,000 ft. per minute, bad things would happen. One night, I recall this monster paper machine nearly vibrated off its moorings. But, persistence, and the excellence of the teams finally paid off. They made enough good product to warrant further commitments to expand the business, with P&G's TAD machines making CPF tissue.

Shane Meeker | How did you feel about becoming Advertising Manager of the Paper Division?

Ed Artzt | Puzzled at first. Enthusiastic after talking to Ed Harness.

I was running Tide at the Brand Promotion Manager level, and we had just finished a great year with a 3 million case volume increase in Tide's 17th year. So I didn't see it as being demoted. Also, I had built a reputation as a fairly decent troubleshooter, dating back to my days as Comet Brand Manager, so I wanted to know what we would all be troubleshooting in the Paper Division. Ed Harness cleared that up in a hurry.

Keep in mind that Ed Harness was probably the brightest and most capable manager in the Company after Morgens. He was certainly a role model and a second father to me, so I didn't need much selling from him to agree to work at his side. But I will never forget that first conversation.

Ed said, "Let me tell you about a conversation I had with Morgens. It started out with Morgens saying you either fix the Paper business, or we are getting out. We have lost over $300 hundred million, and we have nothing to show for it. This is not a business we have to be in, we can still do diapers, but we have to succeed in the tissue business for this whole venture to make financial sense."

Ed responded to Morgens by repeating his deep conviction that the Paper Division could deliver the CPF product at design rates across all of its tissue brands. Ed also reminded Howard that once we completed the scale-up job, P&G would have an insurmountable head start over the competition, mainly Scott. Ed Harness was convinced that Scott would be reluctant to scrap its huge investment in conventional tissue manufacturing capacity in order to try to match P&G's TAD manufacturing technology. We're talking multi-millions in plant and equipment investment in order to channel P&G's entry in the tissue industry.

"Expanding established brands as new brands in a new geography only works when those established brands are healthy and growing in their existing markets."

Ed was right, and Howard Morgens knew Ed would have to have the horses to pull the whole thing off. And that's when he gave Ed Harness the blank check for the people and capital spending that followed. Needless to say, the Soap Divisions' Management screamed bloody murder over losing their people, but Howard stuck to his guns.

From my standpoint, we had several things to fix on the marketing side. We had to learn how to expand geographically in the territories where the trade didn't want P&G in the tissue business and where the competition would throw everything they had at us to keep us from succeeding.

The business had already been separated into two groups. Pampers, which was already expanding nationally, was assigned to the

Bar Soap Division because the tissue brands were still stalled in the old Charmin marketing area — only 37% of the U.S. Paper Division included Charmin, Bounty, Puffs and White Cloud, paper manufacturing and R&D handled Pampers, as well as the tissue products.

Not having the volume of Pampers to bolster the tissue line was a clear disadvantage for any new Paper sales force in new markets. We learned that lesson in our White Cloud and Puffs expansion test market in Texas, where the major trade literally boycotted our tissue brands in protest against P&G entering the business. They feared that P&G's aggressive marketing would eventually result in lower trade pricing and profitability.

Another important lesson comes from the simple fact that expanding established brands as new brands in new geography only works when those established brands are healthy and growing in their existing markets. Otherwise, the trade has all the information they need to withhold their support or even to deny P&G distribution. We learned this earlier in the international business, and we learned it again in Paper, where the situation was made even worse by expanding with an inexperienced sales force recruited from existing P&G sales forces. It was much better to use a strong local P&G sales force like Bar Soap or Food until Paper could eventually be split-off to manage its own brands.

Second, I had to get us ready to introduce CPF tissue on all of our brands. That's a whole different story. My hat is tipped to our Paper advertising people who developed the Whipple advertising and transparent poly packaging for Charmin toilet tissue before I joined them. In fact, the key success with CPF paper was achieved on Charmin toilet tissue. Due to the delayed availability from CPF production, we were able to test market three different elements of the brand's reintroduction in existing markets and initial introduction in new geography. The three elements were CPF tissue, transparent poly packaging (we were first in the industry) and Whipple's "Please don't squeeze the Charmin" advertising. Each of these elements contributed share growth in test markets. I don't remember those numbers, but combined, the synergy produced dramatic results, giving Charmin the vitality it needed to launch successfully as a new brand. For the record, Whipple first aired in 1964 and was a strategy change from "gentle" to "softer."

John Pepper   About what year was this happening, Ed?

Ed Artzt   It was 1965 up to 1968.

John Pepper   OK, because I first met you and first worked for you in 1963. You were in charge of Tide and most of the Soap

Division, as the Brand Promotion Manager position at that time. Then, did you go right into the Paper position?

Ed Artzt | Yes, that's right. I had been in that Soap Division job since 1962, following a two-year stint as manager of the Advertising Copy Section. I had been in the Brand Promotion Manager position in Soap for three years when Ed tapped me for Paper.

John Pepper | Was there an emergency in the Copy Section that was the reason you were sent there?

Ed Artzt | Not really. In 1960, Ed Lotspeich was moved from Copy to Soap Advertising Manager when Ed Harness moved up to head the Soap Products Division. They asked me to follow Ed for a temporary period in which I was asked to determine whether the Copy Section function was still needed, and if so, in what form.

The Copy Section was originally created to facilitate the transition of the bulk of P&G Advertising from radio to television. In the 1940s we found ourselves in the business of making 60-second movies in which we could demonstrate our products, develop continuing characters and add a third dimension of live action visualization to the best communication values of radio and print.

This required a small organization to focus full time on client oversight of our ad agencies and to work with the brand groups to feed the copy development process with performance facts and legally cleared claim support for each product. Copy Supervisors were responsible for making certain each brand's copy execution adhered to the brand's copy strategy.

In a similar internal organization, P&G Productions had been functioning extremely well to provide P&G oversight for the Company's radio soap operas. They continued to perform that

Ed
Lotspeich

"*Ed Lotspeich did a great job of establishing the oversight disciplines that guided the roles of the many functions in the Company that impacted our advertising.*"

function for the television soaps. McElroy and Morgens both believed that excellent staff groups were a competitive edge for P&G, and they had encouraged the creation of these kinds of functions throughout the Company.

Ed Lotspeich did a great job of establishing the oversight disciplines that guided the roles of the many functions in the Company that impacted our advertising. Those functions included: the Brand Groups, Product Development, the Legal Section, the Commercial Production Section, the Art Section and in the middle, Advertising Copy Management. Lotspeich also recruited and trained a talented group of copy specialists like Norm Levy, Gib Carey and Dick McKinney. McKinney extended the copy function to International by relocating in Brussels, but instead of creating a bunch of Copy Sections overseas, Dick's job was to train Brand Managers in foreign countries to perform the Copy Management functions the P&G way.

> *The guiding principle behind the Copy Section's mission was to respond to an Agency's creative work with "one voice" in detail and in writing. It made a lot of sense; because "mixed signals" had been the Agencies' number one complaint about working with P&G people on developing new advertising.*

I really enjoyed the Copy Management job and learned a lot from it. I finally concluded that the responsibility for approving advertising should be given to the Brand Groups, and that the Copy Supervisors should be assigned to Divisions in order to provide expert advice and training — and this is what we did.

Splitting the responsibility for advertising strategy and execution was not permanently viable. Too many "cooks" had created internal tension over the years, especially when a brand was perceived to be in copy trouble. During those times, Brand Groups wanted to play the leading role with their Agencies to get better advertising for their ailing business.

The Brand Groups resented being distanced from the creative execution process at the Agency. They wanted to be in charge, but often, they had to wait for the Copy Section and Agency to bring them presentations for their approval, and many of our Brand Managers did not like being reminded that "you do strategy, and we do execution."

But what was worse, neither Toilet Goods nor Paper had Copy Supervisors assigned to them, so the Brand Managers in Soap and Food felt like they had less to say about advertising copy than their colleagues in other advertising departments.

The Copy Section had outlived its original purpose of transitioning the Company's advertising expertise from radio to TV. But the need to advise and train P&G and Agency people in the Copy Management process remained, and we kept that going.

The organizational division between Copy and Brand was only a small part of the seismic change that was taking place throughout the Company during Howard Morgen's tenure as CEO from 1957-1974. Howard's strategic vision was to convert P&G from a U.S. Soap and Shortening Company into a broadly diversified international business, but he felt that the Company was not moving fast enough.

The bottleneck was our organizational structure, and he changed it dramatically by divisionalizing the Company's staff groups. To do that, he created five Operating Divisions and eliminated the functional silos that had isolated Brand Management from Product Development, Sales and Manufacturing. The Vice-Presidents in charge of these functions became staff Vice-Presidents, and most of their people were transferred to the operating divisions to support the day-to-day business.

The blueprint for Howard's restructuring plan undoubtedly originated during his earlier days in Toilet Goods. Howard, as I said earlier, agreed to become Toilet Goods Manager only if he was also given responsibility for the functional groups he needed to run the business. In any case, all of these changes created opportunities for Paper to piggyback on larger, more mature sales forces, at least until Paper could complete U.S. expansion. It also created additional tension internally.

John Pepper	Do you remember if it was Bar Soap or Toilet Goods? I know it was a different division.
Ed Artzt	I am almost certain it was the Bar Soap Division. I know they were chosen to handle Pampers, and they did a pretty good job. I also think the Company used Bar Soap to expand our tissue brands, including Bounty, outside the Charmin marketing area. Bounty Brand Management was in Paper. Pampers was not. Complicated, but in the end, it worked because of the ability of P&G people to work together in the midst of chaos.
Shane Meeker	So the trade didn't want us in Paper, but then internally, our own sales organization also was kind of struggling moving into Paper.
Ed Artzt	Remember, the trade didn't want P&G in the disposables business for profitability reasons. The Bar Soap Division did not like being the surrogate for the birth of the Paper Division, because they knew that someday they would have to give up the disposables brands. They saw themselves as agents with struggling brands in the tissue categories, competing with two icon brands, Scott tissue and Kleenex. They griped, but they never dragged their feet.

As for the two sales options, we tested both, piggybacking and starting a Paper sales force from scratch in new markets, and piggybacking was best, hands down.

This would be a good time, John, to return to the subject of Pampers and shape, or the ill-advised decision to give shaped diapers to a second brand, Luvs. How do smart people do that? I have studied this subject a lot because it's full of valuable lessons for the Company going forward.

Let me start by reviewing where we were when we were confronted with the need to make a major product decision on our diaper business. Namely, whether to introduce our shaped diaper as a premium-priced Pampers flanker, or as a new brand, Luvs.

1. We had a successful Pampers business based on high-speed production of a Z-fold rectangular diaper. The product's main vulnerability was its fit. It leaked. It also was a significant blind test loser to our own shaped diaper, and blind testing warned of the possible consequences. In response to direct questioning, a third of the women who tried our shaped diaper said they would be willing to pay up to a 30% premium to buy it. Those Pampers users were prime candidates to switch to Huggies in the absence of a Pampers entry.

2. At that point in time, we were well ahead of Kimberly-Clark in the race to introduce shaped diapers, but our initial product required slow-speed converting, and it was costly to make. It would have to be premium priced and could not utilize existing Z-fold diaper manufacturing capacity. Therefore, the more a shaped Pampers might cannibalize regular Pampers, the bigger our scrapping bill would be.

3. P&G had a history in the laundry business of offering consumers new benefits in new or repositioned brands rather

than by extending Tide's product line to protect its franchise. For example, Cheer got bluing, Oxydol got bleach, Bold got fabric softener and Dash got low suds. At one point, I recall we had seven laundry brands, and Tide was just Tide. We were lucky that none of these add-on brands were performance game changers, or Tide might have suffered the same fate as Pampers.

The decision to withhold shape from Pampers and use it on a second brand instead was not only wrong, it also proved to be disastrous for the brand. Pampers lost its leadership of the category in the U.S. to Huggies, a brand that didn't even exist at the time of the decision. All that Kimberly-Clark had at that point was a struggling Kimbies brand.

I am not sure of all the thinking that went into the Luvs versus Pampers shape decision. I was not directly responsible for Pampers until I moved to Europe in 1975. But I am aware of much of the debate that took place and some of the thinking that tipped the balance. Much of what I learned came from my frequent talks with Ed Harness, who was both my boss in Paper and the Senior Officer in charge of the Pampers business.

So, where did we go wrong? I suspect that financial pressure may have prevailed in the end because of the operating losses and capital spending requirements that the Paper Division was undergoing in the 1960s. However, mistaken assumptions figured heavily in the decision. There were three big ones:

1. We grossly miscalculated what Kimberly-Clark's strategy would be in response to a P&G-shaped diaper entry. Our people expected Kimberly to follow our Pampers' lead by introducing a secondary premium-shaped diaper while keeping Kimbies as a direct competitor to Pampers.

Kimberly-Clark did just the opposite. They adopted the strategy that Coach Bill Belichick uses to win Patriots games — "Define your opponent's weaknesses and attack them." The diaper market was small, only 3.5 million births annually in 1965, and the number of homes with children in diapers turned over completely every two years. So Kimberly was well aware of the need to capture a major share of its business from Pampers in order to succeed financially. So, in 1978, after several years of test marketing alongside Kimbies, Kimberly-Clark introduced its hourglass-shaped Huggies diaper as a complete replacement for Kimbies. Pampers had been blindsided.

2. We misinterpreted the consumer research that told us one-third of new mothers would pay a 30% premium for shaped Pampers. What the research was really telling us, between the lines, was that virtually all new mothers would buy shaped Pampers if it weren't premium priced. We evidently dismissed the possibility that future cost and manufacturing efficiencies would eliminate the need for premium pricing, making Z-fold rectangular obsolete. This, of course, is what happened.

"Never give a consumer a product reason to switch away from your brand, especially if it's the market leader."

3. Finally, and perhaps most importantly, our technical people argued convincingly that shaped diapers would always require premium pricing because of the inherent manufacturing inefficiency. However, their projections were all based on past experience with small-scale test market equipment that had operated at line speeds of up to 160 pads per minute versus over 400 pads per minute for Z-fold Pampers.

They should have said, "What if" we could scale up shaped Pampers to 400 pads per minute, which they eventually did. "What if" Kimberly converts to shape? Is Luvs going to be a strong enough stalking horse to protect Pampers? It was not. These questions alone should have supported test marketing shaped Pampers as a premium-priced flanker, until the shaped product eventually converted 100% of Pampers business. Instead, we chose a strategic path that caused us to be four years behind Huggies with national sale of shaped Pampers.

The Pampers shaped product decision was a bitter and costly one, but it gave us lessons for the future that I hope won't be lost. In fact, we created P&G College to preserve and communicate those experiences; I used three of them in my lecture to employees on product deployment strategies. I would like to restate them here for the record.

1. Never give the consumer a product reason to switch away from your brand, especially if it is the market leader. The market-place teaches us that one multi-version mega-brand has more longevity potential than several mini-brands, each tied to a single generic benefit like bleach in Oxydol and shape on Luvs.

2. If you are first to market with a breakthrough in technology, don't expect your competition to do what you do; they will copy your technology in the way that helps them and hurts you the most. Kimberly-Clark did just that.

"Never base your future projections of technical progress on past performance on pilot equipment. Always ask 'what if' we could beat these numbers."

	3. Never base your future projections of technical progress on past performance on pilot equipment. Ask, "what if" we could beat these numbers. Would we follow a different plan? If the answer is "maybe, yes," then test market the alternatives. I firmly believe that if we had tested shaped Pampers as a premium-priced companion to our national Pampers product, it would have been a clear winner over the Luvs alternative. And, we would have beaten Huggies timing and protected Pampers leadership position.
John Pepper	Well, the lecture you always gave contained memorable phrases. They are still taught in the halls and can certainly be applied here on Pampers as well as others. We gave people an abundant reason to switch. So many things apply to that basic point.
Ed Artzt	Other things do apply as our Tide Liquid experience tells us. I recall the Laundry Products Division recommended test marketing Tide Liquid back in the 70s, even though the product did not match Tide's cleaning performance. That first iteration was turned down by CEO Ed Harness because of his strong feelings about the Tide cleaning franchise. I believe that I was running

Europe at the time, but I remember Ed Harness telling me, "I am never going to let this Company introduce a brand with the name Tide on it that doesn't clean as well as our powder Tide."

I was skeptical, but I didn't argue with him then because I didn't know how bad our liquid was or why he felt so strongly about it. I know that Ed Harness, like many P&G leaders before him, was opposed in principle to marketing product flankers on brands like Tide because of the danger of diluting the brand's franchise with consumers.

Our product people eventually got us a much better performing Tide Liquid. By the time it was introduced nationally in 1984, John Smale had already succeeded Ed, and Unilever's Wisk had grown into a much stronger competitor.

Wisk had been hanging around since 1956 and was sold for years as a pre-treater. But in 1968 it aired its "Ring Around the Collar" ad campaign and started growing until it reached about an 8% share of the laundry category. P&G countered Luvs-style with two minor brand-stalking horses, Era in 1972 and Solo in 1975. But those brands are gone, and Tide Liquid eventually overtook Wisk.

In this case, Ed was right. We had allowed Tide to give consumers a product reason to switch brands, but not many of them did.

Why the exception? I have come to believe that these outcomes depend on how good the competitor's product is. Wisk was no Huggies, and it never matched Tide powder in cleaning performance. Also, just as Huggies cut deeply into Pampers, Unilever's Dove separately damaged our Ivory business because Dove had patented a better product than Ivory. We did not have a synthetic Ivory formula that was good enough to avoid Dove's patents and match or beat Dove's performance. Ivory stayed the course and really took it on the chin.

Looking back, I wish we had included the Tide Liquid history in our P&G College lectures. The importance of neither under-estimating nor overestimating the dimensions of a competitor's threat to our business is worth a lot of study. We are still getting blindsided by strategic errors of omission. Look at how Gillette's failure to quickly counter the threat from shave clubs resulted in heavy business losses.

John Pepper

You know, you touched on the lessons in P&G College, and I wonder if you would be willing to say a word about P&G College. You started P&G College. We had train-ing. I have been through that training, but we never had it formulated as a College with everything linked to it. Could you talk about what led you to take that organization step?

Ed Artzt

I wanted to find a way to encourage our management to do what

Jerry
Dirvin

I was doing, namely, training our employees by sharing my own personal experiences with them. I felt we were losing touch with P&G's cultural roots. P&G College was a possible way to restore that connection and the practical learning that went with it, and to pass it along with what I had learned from my Company elders.

John Pepper | Did you get any resistance to it?

Ed Artzt | Not that I ever heard about. Jerry Dirvin helped me put it together, and he did a good job of generating acceptance. He knew that P&G management people would enjoy talking about the Company's history — good and bad. They would also like talking about their own experiences. The attendance was so good that we eventually moved it out of the building to its own location in the downtown training center.

John Pepper | I believe you mentioned earlier the idea came in part from a book Jerry Dirvin gave you.

Ed Artzt | Yes. It was called, "The Leadership Secrets of Attila the Hun." It was intended as a joke, but it contained one central theme that made an impression on me. The culture of a tribe is passed on for generations by gatherings around the campfire. That is when the elders pass along their knowledge to the upcoming generation of future leaders. It's a time to tell stories, share experiences and transmit wisdom behind the tribe's guiding principles. The campfire is essential to the group's longevity.

Now, Attila was no role model for any civilized group to emulate, but the concept in the book was an allegorical description of parenting where the elders, your parents, prepare you for adulthood around the dinner table, instead of around a campfire. When I finished the book, I realized that P&G had done just that at the daily luncheons in the old Executive Dining Room at the P&G office in the Gwynne Building.

I was fortunate to have been elected to the Company's Administrative Committee while we were still in the old building and still meeting daily in the Executive Dining Room. It was a remarkable experience. I was amazed at how much you can learn from just hanging around these men and listening to them talk about the Company.

The lunch hour was a ritual. There were rules for attendance, decorum and discussion. First, if you were in Cincinnati, you were expected to be at lunch and be there on time. You were also expected to be there wearing matching suit and tie. If you were a junior officer, as I was, you did not initiate the discussion topics. Messrs, Dupree, McElroy and Morgens did that. We listened, and of course, answered their questions when asked. As a rookie, I

Rowell Chase

was expected to supply Mr. Dupree's place setting with his favorite brand of cigarettes and Mr. Rowell Chase, ditto with his cigars.

The atmosphere was cordial, not stiff, but lunchtime was designed to be a very efficient version of a tribal campfire. I loved it, and I learned a great deal from hearing the three former P&G Chieftains share their knowledge of our history and their wisdom as the Company's decision-makers.

It was also a time for informal discussions of the business, quite different from the Administrative Committee or Board meetings. We all learned important news about the business, political developments and news about the Cincinnati community. But the main purpose of these daily lunch gatherings was to teach the younger generation of managers how the Company thinks about things and why our guiding principles are always going to be tested by the world we work in. So we ought to know these principles. We ought to live by them, and we ought to want to pass them on to our successors. I was one of the younger generations of managers in the Company, but so were Ed Harness and John Smale. Imagine that.

There I was having lunch every day with the people that led the Company throughout its modern history, and I quickly discovered that when you have a chance to hear them face up, during work and sometimes after work, you are going to learn things about P&G that you would have never otherwise learned. Then all of a sudden, the Company became too big, too busy, too geographically diverse, and the daily gathering tradition died.

We created P&G College in order to restore that tradition in a way capable of reaching virtually all of our future managers. Also, instead of casual discussion, we created case histories based on

"Above all my mentors, Ed Harness filled me with his passion for winning. He taught me how to think strategically to win against our major business competition. Ed was a warrior."

real events — case histories that provided significant lessons for the future. And we recruited our active Company executives to serve as the P&G College training instructors.

John Pepper
> You mentioned Ed Harness, I know he had a big impact on you. What was it you think you took away from your relationship with Ed Harness?

Ed Artzt
Ed Harness, above all of my mentors, filled me with his passion for winning and taught me how to think strategically in order to win against our major business competition. Ed was a warrior, and his obsession rubbed off on his subordinates, me included.

Ed had another valuable trait that he imparted to everyone under him. He believed that all decisions on the business should be addressed first and foremost on the basis of the principle involved. He always preached the value of defining the principle in every recommendation. Practicality, affordability, risk, benefit and all other important considerations were second to the principle involved, in Ed's mind. He believed it. He managed by it, and he pounded it into his troops. I can still remember him starting off a discussion of my recommendations with the question, "What's the principle involved here?" After a while, you always answered the question before he asked it, and you realized it was an invaluable guide to management thinking.

I want to add that I had several exceptional mentors at P&G. Bill Snow early on, and Bill Gurganus, who I succeeded in International. Both were wonderfully tough taskmaster bosses. However, Ed Harness and John Smale topped the list. Ed was like my father. John Smale was like my older brother.

Ed Harness was one of the brightest men I have ever known. At the same time, he was a down-to-earth, small-town guy who exuded warmth and a clever wit in his relationships with people. Ed

John Smale (standing)
& Ed Artzt

grew up in Marietta, Ohio. His father owned the local newspaper, where Ed learned to be a skillful communicator. People who
worked for Ed didn't just like him; we loved the man. During
WWII, Ed served in the U.S. Air Force for four years, during
which he rose from Lieutenant to Major. Ed was a natural leader
wherever he was.

Ed also was a master at preparation, another skill he helped me
hone. Ed was a genius at preparing for the demands of his job,
and you had better be prepared whenever you were meeting with
Ed on an important business issue.

Ed Harness's greatest legacy as a senior P&G Executive was
undoubtedly his strategic leadership of the Paper business. He
will of course always be remembered for his decision in 1980 to
discontinue Rely Tampons nationally amidst concerns about a
possible connection to toxic shock syndrome after only five years
on the market. The introduction and withdrawal of Rely took
place while I was working in Europe, and I had no personal experience with him on that project during that time.

While the results on our tissue business have been mixed
throughout the years, Ed gets the lion's share of the credit from
the fact that we entered four major disposables categories, and
we achieved market leadership on three of the four brands in the
U.S. — Pampers, Charmin and Bounty, plus global leadership
on Pampers. Only Puffs facial tissue, in the number two position,
failed to overtake the number one U.S. brand, Kleenex.

Since then of course, the Company returned to the feminine
hygiene business with Always/Whisper, and I believe P&G now
has global leadership in that market as well.

When Howard Morgens transferred Ed from the Soap Division
to Paper in 1963, Ed faced the difficult task of convincing the

P&G Board that we should invest more millions of dollars in tissue manufacturing capacity. We had entered this very capital-intensive market without a superior product we knew how to make. Ed couldn't know whether we would ever succeed to scale up CPF Tissue successfully, but his coolness under pressure while everyone else was sweating bullets was inspiring. His strategy had the potential to obsolesce the rest of the industry's tissue products and give us a several-year head start with Charmin nationally.

The scale-up of P&G's CPF tissue-making capacity was a challenge that might never have succeeded were it not for Ed's hands-on management skills. During the toughest days of the Mehoopany startup, Ed exhibited a knowledge of the technology, and a degree of confidence in his people and their mission, which served as an example to all of us. It was a great learning experience to serve under such a capable leader, and those lessons stay with you.

Ed's convictions were right, Scott was forced to undertake a major capital investment in TAD tissue manufacturing equipment, but they were 10 years behind Charmin. By 1995, Scott was heavily indebted by the tissue capacity investment burden, coupled with risky investments in overseas expansion in new business categories. Scott was broken up and sold off. Most of its consumer brands went to Kimberly-Clark.

P&G, meanwhile, tested and successfully expanded Always/Whisper, our feminine hygiene entry in the U.S. in 1984 and in multiple foreign countries starting in 1985. The Company market tested, but eventually gave up its plans for expanding tissue products into Europe, meanwhile acquiring Tampax tampons globally in 1997.

Another lesson I learned from Ed Harness was that beating the competition required a clear understanding of how you were going to do it, not just the intent. After all, if you are going to enter a mature market against entrenched competition, that is where your business has to come from. You have to be aware of what they might do and how quickly they can neutralize your basis for entry — and your product's advantage.

In Paper, the dominant brand was Scott Tissue; they had half the business. It was beat them or go home. So, Ed kept us all focused on that necessity. I know it helped me, because I had never felt good about tackling something really difficult until I had some idea of who we had to beat and how we were going to beat them.

John Pepper

You always talked to International about measuring how well we were going to be doing by how good our General Managers were compared to a competitor's General Manager.

Ed Artzt

Yes. I have always believed that matchups can influence outcomes in business just as they do in team sports. This is especially true with International subsidiaries where the General Managers are closely involved with local sales promotion, pricing, advertising copy, trade merchandising and even product assortment. It takes the right people in the right jobs at the right time to win in a large global business like ours.

In order to manage that process successfully, it pays to know the strengths and weaknesses of the managers running the competition's brands and businesses. For example, I can recall when I was Brand Manager on Comet, I had a pretty good knowledge of my counterpart's tendencies on Ajax. As a result, we were ready to take advantage of his mistakes whenever he made them, and he did. So did we, and he made us pay as well.

We also had a different kind of example in Switzerland.

John Pepper

Yes. That would be one of many. Remind us.

Ed Artzt | Bill Gurganus and I were making our first tour through several smaller countries in Europe that had been managed as export markets reporting to King Fletcher. Some of them had become part of the newly formed European Common Market, so they were added to my group of European countries. They were also being run on the ground by Country Managers who did not have the depth of management expertise that you would find in most P&G International Subsidiaries.

Bill Gurganus understood the situation. He was a gentleman, but he was not a patient man. In fact, he would just turn purple at some of the dumb things people would say about the business as we toured the circuit. Finally, in Switzerland, Bill had to let off some steam. The recipient was a former Copy Supervisor and amateur Shakespearean actor from the UK, whose business in Switzerland was in decline. Our Country Manager didn't know much. When he was asked to explain what was wrong, he stumbled through a very bad answer, until he finally revealed that all the trouble started when Unilever brought in a different General Manager, a young guy who was regarded as up-and-coming in their company. By that time, Gurganus was bursting at the seams. I could see the blood vessels on his head were about to pop, and he spoke just a few words with a strained smile on his face. He said, "It is a testimony to your great ability as a Copy man that your business is no worse than it is." Our Country Manager, thinking it was a compliment, said, "Thank you, Mr. Gurganus."

Our man found himself mismatched versus his counterpart at Unilever, a young stud whose aggressive actions were not being adequately analyzed or challenged by P&G, and we were losing share on our core brands. I felt sorry for the guy, but we had no choice but to appoint a stronger manager in Switzerland as soon as possible.

A similar matchup change occurred in Austria. That time it worked in P&G's favor when we promoted Durk Jager to his first Country Manager job there as part of his fast-track career development.

John Pepper

One thing I wanted to ask you as we get into this history: There is a story you told me last time I was here, and that was about your start with P&G coming from Los Angeles. You were there on sales training. Maybe talk a little bit about that, about how you got there and that fabled trip across the country, and then about afterward as you were asked to give a report of what you discovered. This has to be in this oral history.

Ed Artzt

OK. I graduated from the University of Oregon with a degree in journalism in 1951. My wife and I moved to Los Angeles where I had grown up. My mother lived there, and I also had some connections there. I didn't know what I wanted to do, so I got a job in the three career areas that I had some interest in: newspaper writing, television production and advertising.

I was fortunate enough to get three jobs which allowed me to test all three possible career directions at the same time. I got a job in the morning working for a daily newspaper, where I got to do some sports writing, which I love. I got a job in the afternoon working for a local advertising agency. They hired me as a copywriter, and, except for college, I had never written a word of advertising copy in my life. The third job had me working for a TV production company that owned a couple of local TV shows in Los Angeles. My position was called Production Assistant, and I was responsible for getting costumes, sets and participants ready for each weekly telecast.

I worked all three jobs for a year until I concluded the career I had the most passion for was advertising account management, preferably in a large agency on the East Coast, where most of them were headquartered. Just as I was about to embark on my

East Coast search, fate stepped in with a little help from my Uncle Charlie. Yes, I had an Uncle Charlie living in Los Angeles. He was a retired automotive engineer from Detroit, and he was aware of my job search. He also was the only one I knew who noticed P&G's recruiting ad in the Los Angeles Times. When he brought the ad to our apartment, I remember him saying, "This Brand Management sounds like what you are looking for."

Luckily for me, P&G had decided to do some West Coast recruiting. At that time, P&G's idea of West Coast recruiting was to run a full-page ad in the LA Times, followed by a screening interview visit by a P&G HR staffer, Sid Johnson. The P&G ad was quite good. To me, Brand Management sounded like the client side of Advertising Account Management — only better. So I answered the ad and was invited to the Los Angeles office of one of P&G's ad agencies, Dancer, Fitzgerald and Sample, to take a test. I must have passed P&G's test because they then sent me a letter saying, "We are interested in talking to you, and we are inviting you to come to Cincinnati for interviews."

Wonderful, but except for Sid Johnson, I still had not met anyone from the Company. So when I arrived in Cincinnati, I had no idea that I would be seeing all of the top people in the Advertising department. I remember being interviewed by Bill Snow, Ed Harness, Pete Link, Bill Gurganus, Tom Warrington, Dick Oster and Hal Payne, all in one day. It was overwhelming. These people were really smart, and they took the hiring process very seriously. It's the reason I put so much effort into recruiting when I was CEO.

John Pepper   Those were the top managers in the group at that time?

Ed Artzt   Yes, and they all worked me over thoroughly. But the interview I remember best was the one with Hal Payne. He was an Associate Advertising Manager and the youngest of my interviewers that day.

Hal Payne sat there tapping his pencil throughout the interview, and I remember thinking this guy is a nervous wreck. I was getting nervous myself when Hal asked me, "How's your mathematics?" I said, "What mathematics are you talking about?" I told him that I had already been asked once that day whether I had taken differential calculus in school. I said I couldn't even spell it, let alone take it. Hal said, "Don't worry about it; all you need here is seventh-grade arithmetic." I knew that wasn't true, but it relaxed me because I also knew that I had been pretty good at seventh-grade arithmetic.

The day ended with my receiving a job offer on the spot, which I accepted a few days later after getting my wife's agreement to move to Cincinnati. At that point, I was 23. She was 22, and we had a 2-year-old daughter and a second one on the way. Because of my young family, and marketing experience in LA, P&G let me start in Sales Training so that we wouldn't have to move twice — first to Cincinnati as a Brand Assistant, then back into a Sales District for six months of training before returning as an Assistant Brand Manager. The Company actually hired me as an Assistant Brand Manager in Sales Training. That example of the Company's concern about the treatment of employees' families made a deep and lasting impression on me.

Sales Training was a valuable experience for me. It was a huge reality check of the Company's relationships with its trade customers, especially the policies that our Sales organization had to enforce in their day-to-day work. Basically, the trade disliked P&G because we were unbending on matters of policy. For example, we wouldn't mis-redeem coupons. We would not pay under the table for displays or features, and we would charge everyone the same price and give everyone the same volume discounts on our brands, whether the customer was large or small. Los Angeles was one of the toughest trade environments in the country, a good place to break in a rookie like me.

From the very beginning, though, I could see that relations between the Company's Sales and adverting departments were strained. I was treated very well by the Sales people in Los Angeles partly because I was a new Sales employee, not a transferred Brand guy from Cincinnati. Still, there was one incident during my Sales assignment that demonstrated how bureaucratic thinking in Cincinnati could discourage teamwork and individual initiative between the two long-siloed functions.

It all started when our District Manager called his sales team together and told us that we had been challenged by Pacific Division Sales Management to come up with some advertising ideas that would help increase our featuring by chain accounts. Our LA district was running behind the rest of the country in this measure of performance. Key account featuring covered the inclusion of P&G Brands in a large chain account's weekly ad. This usually included an overall theme plus a temporary cut-in price and mass displays of the advertised products in stores. We were not getting much support in LA, because you had to pay extra cash discounts to get that. P&G had a standard rate per case for featuring and displays, but it was not enough money to subsidize cut-price featuring. We also provided newspaper mats of our brands to be used in trade ads, but there was nothing new available to us at the time to overcome all the barriers. We needed a fresh idea.

So, in my youthful enthusiasm, I came up with one. It was a banner for a trade ad with the headline, "P&G Washday Sale." Underneath the headline was a clothesline with pictures of babies that I cut out from our Ivory bar soap wrappers. Each baby was clutching a P&G brand. I think the brands at that time were Tide, Oxydol, Ivory Snow, Dreft and Ivory Bar Soap, but I'm not certain. In order to enable our Sales group to present this promotion theme to the trade, I asked my art director friend at my former ad agency employer to prepare some line drawing artwork and produce about 100 newspaper mats. They did that work as a favor to me, so it cost P&G nothing.

Our District sales team loved it, and they sold literally dozens of "P&G Washday Sales" to our normally hostile trade customers. In fact, our District Manager liked it so much he sent samples of the ads to Cincinnati, suggesting that other Sales Districts might want to use it too. That's when it hit the fan.

The messenger was my staff contact in the Advertising Department in Cincinnati. Instead of saying, "Good going. Your Sales District is pleased with your work," he delivered a reprimand. His message was, "Cool it, kid. Cincinnati Sales Management doesn't want Advertising trainees to display skills or use resources that are not available to the average salesman." In other words, keep your head down, your mouth shut and don't do anything to cause the Sales people to wonder if they are at a disadvantage to Advertising people. It was a sensitive subject. Remember, "You are there to learn, not to stir up interdepartmental jealousies." These may not have been his exact words, but that sure was the message. Needless to say, I was shocked, and he wasn't through.

My Advertising Department contact went on to say that I had baby illustrations which were used on the back and sides of the Large Size Ivory Soap wrapper. Maybe so, I thought, but these were P&G property, and so was the "P&G Washday Sale" banner. The babies in my ad were holding P&G packages. Logos also were copyrighted and regularly used in trade ads. I bristled at that message, too, but I didn't argue the legal question. Rather, I remember thinking that P&G Staff was using its internal bureaucracy to discourage individual initiative. This may have been a necessary protection, but it sends a frustrating message, "Don't make waves. You may be stepping on other people's turf."

John Pepper	How old were you at the time?
Ed Artzt	Twenty-four. I was 23 when I joined the Company. I think I had only been with P&G a few months.
John Pepper	So just when you were starting the job?
Ed Artzt	Yes, and later when I returned to Cincinnati, it became even clearer that "turf" was a major internal problem in our Company. Even as an Assistant Brand Manager, I could see why Howard Morgens had refused to take the Toilet Goods job unless he had all of the line resources he needed reporting directly to him.
John Pepper	So, Toilet Goods was really ahead of Soap in reporting to one person?
Ed Artzt	Absolutely. The Company created its first Division, the Drug Products Division in 1943, with Howard as its manager. Soap didn't follow until 1955 when Howard divisionalized the whole Company. By the way, John Smale spent his early years in the Drug Products structure.

There was more to this historical event than just the adoption of Morgens' untraditional organization structure. It was all about a strategic need to develop successful brands in the Toilet Goods business. P&G had entered the hair care segment with Drene Shampoo way back in 1934, and while we had a number of product initiatives in various stages of development, the business wasn't developing very well.

Deupree and McElroy wanted to exploit the opportunity they thought we had in shampoos, home permanents, dentifrices and skincare, so they reached for their strongest manager, Morgens. Howard knew from his frustrations in Soap that the walls between Brand Management and Product Development in particular would pose impenetrable bottlenecks to the rapid marketing startup of new Toilet Goods brands. So, he told his bosses, "I will have to be in charge of all the Toilet Goods Departments, or I won't be able to make this work." So they gave Howard what he wanted, and that's where the seeds of structural change at P&G took root.

The conflict between the Company's functional silos actually began much earlier — in 1931, when Neal McElroy and RR Deupree hatched the Brand Management system. The original purpose was to better manage competition between the brands, and it did. But it also created competition between P&G departments, which over time became a serious obstacle to progress for the group of newly created Brand Managers, most notably among them, Howard Morgens.

The deep silos in Product Development, Sales and Manufacturing were handicapping Brand Groups at every turn. It is fair to say that the new Brand Management system was not well received within the Company's various functional communities. It was considered a threat to their autonomy, and rules were passed to make it as difficult as possible for Brand Managers to influence all parts of the business on their brands.

Brand Managers were perceived as young cowboys, fresh out of business school, who would surely mess up things if allowed to run loose amidst the Product Groups, Trade Customers, Sales Districts or P&G factories. We were even seen as being disdainful of traditional P&G rules of dress, wearing two-toned shoes and sports jackets and slacks to work. In response, the Advertising Department formalized its own dress code to simply avoid being disrespected by the silos we needed to penetrate.

Unfortunately, Company recruiting ads and materials didn't help matters when they described Brand Managers as Presidents of their own small Companies, which of course, was a gross exaggeration. But, it encouraged the functional managers at P&G to respond as if to say, "We'll be dammed if we're going to let that happen."

We owe Howard Morgens a huge debt of gratitude for his willingness to buck the system back in1943. We also owe a similar debt to RR Deupree and Neal McElroy for making silos-busting happen.

The urgency that Howard Morgens displayed throughout his career was endemic to P&G's culture. A remarkable thing about the Company has been its ability to reinvent itself in the face of imminent obsolescence. Imagine if one of your two core businesses, candles, is replaced by the electric light bulb, and then several decades later, the other half, laundry soaps, is replaced by synthetic detergents. It's no secret that P&G's longevity is a result of a continuing commitment to product innovation. At P&G, you don't just plan for obsolescence, you work to make it happen, and when it does, you want to be the first to market the product answer.

Another example: Cincinnati had been a major hog-rendering market, supplying the Company with tallow for candles and soap. But, when the invention of the cotton gin made it feasible to substitute cottonseed oil for animal fat, P&G acquired seed crushing mills and invented Crisco, the first all-vegetable shortening. Product invention is part of P&G's DNA. Further, the consistent pressing need for invention and the difficulty of achieving it made organizational obstruction all the more oppressive to a visionary like Morgens.

John Pepper	I want to take us back to Los Angeles and have you take us through your trip to Cincinnati with your wife and the two kids.
Ed Artzt	OK. The Company decided that I should return from Sales training during the period of Sales vacations and factory shut down,

which took place during the first two weeks in July for the entire U.S. Sales and Manufacturing forces. My wife's parents had just bought us a new Nash Rambler, a mini-sized car, and we decided to take a week to drive to Cincinnati. There were four of us. Our two daughters were 2 1/2 and 1. It was the hottest summer in years, and I recall that it was 103 degrees in Cincinnati when we got there.

Anyway, there were events leading up to our trip that made me want to check grocery stores as we drove across the country. I learned later that our financial people had notified Howard Morgens that the amended volume forecast for the fourth quarter of our fiscal year would produce a profit windfall that might distort earnings results between fiscal years. Howard was asked if he could spend some of the windfall profit to help stimulate our business in the coming fiscal year. Howard called his managers together, and they decided to use the funds to conduct a national coupon mailing at the end of June, just ahead of Sales and Manufacturing vacations.

"At P&G, you don't just plan for obsolescence, you work to make it happen, and when it does, you'll want to be the first to market the product answer."

I don't recall the brands, but the assortment varied in different parts of the country. I believe our new shampoo, Prell, was couponed everywhere, plus one or two laundry brands and a bar soap.

Of course I didn't know any of this at the time, but all of us in Sales worried that the trade would run out of stock on the couponed brands during shutdown, and there would be no way to replenish them during that two-week period. That was already happening in Los Angeles before I started our trip because my District Manager told me, "We're getting calls from all our accounts. They're out of Tide because when they run out of stock on the couponed brands, consumers redeem their coupons or mis-redeem them on Tide." He said that trade customers considered it our fault for mailing coupons that were redeemable on brands we couldn't make or ship during the peak redemption period because we were both shut down and on vacation.

I found a similar picture in most of the stores I checked across the country. I believe that I logged about 100 stores in total, mostly quick in and out. Even so, that was tough on my wife and kids because of the heat. I'm lucky nobody got heat stroke sitting in supermarket parking lots. Looking back, I regret I put them through that.

When we got back to Cincinnati, I told my boss about my store-check findings. The news evidently traveled fast up the ladder of bosses, and the next thing I knew, I was called up to Howard Morgens office along with either Rowell Chase or Bill Snow. I can't recall which one escorted me there, but it was just one.

John Pepper   This is your first time in Cincinnati?

Ed Artzt   Second time, if you count my one day of job interviews six months earlier.

Howard Morgens welcomed me back from Sales training, and acknowledged that he knew that I had checked a lot of stores on my trip, and he asked me, "What did you find out?"

I told Howard that I found that the couponing was well supported by the trade with features and displays, and redemption appeared to be heavy. But, I also found widespread out of stocks on the couponed brands due to the unfortunate timing. Our Sales people were on vacation, and our factories were shut down for annual maintenance and vacations. Consequently, we were unable to meet trade requests for replenishment of store stocks in a timely fashion. Also mis-redemption seemed to be a problem too. I remember telling him, "I'm sorry, Mr. Morgens, but I don't think we should have mailed those coupons when we did because they arrived when we were unable to replenish stocks of our brands either to warehouses or directly to the larger chain stores." I don't recall Howard's response, but I'm sure we didn't repeat that mistake again.

I was called up to Howard's office again a couple of years later, about six weeks after I had been promoted to Brand Manager on Comet Cleanser. This was different from the time that I had just returned from Sales training. I was summoned because I was responsible for a business that hadn't been doing well, and Howard wanted to know if I shared his sense of urgency about fixing it.

I remember being nervous at first, but my boss, Bill Snow, helped keep me calm. Bill was a contemporary of Howard's. They both joined the Company in 1932, and I could see that they were good friends.

Nevertheless, I knew this was not the normal protocol for meeting with the Chief Executive. There were four levels of management between Howard Morgens and me, and only one of those, Bill Snow, was in the room with me. Bill was two levels above me, so my immediate boss was among the missing. I remember hoping the others above me were OK with me going alone with Bill Snow to meet Howard. There had been no agenda, no advanced notice and no questions to address. Just, "Howard would like to talk to you."

Howard greeted us and said to me, "What should we do?" I looked at my boss, Bill Snow, and said, "I have only been on the brand for six weeks." Bill said, "Go ahead. Tell him." Fortunately, I had just spent the whole weekend preparing an analysis of the Comet expansion results and possible remedial action, so I knew exactly what to tell him.

First, I reminded him that Comet was up against a 60-share monster competitor in Ajax Cleanser. We had a superior 2 to 1 blind test winner in Comet, but we were premium priced and smelled like chlorine bleach. So, it was critical that we sample consumers to obtain trial in homes with porous porcelain sinks, where our Comet stain removal advantage was most decisive. Meanwhile, Colgate employed a trial-blocking defense consisting of loading promotions to delay trial of Comet while they were test-marketing their own chlorinated cleanser as a companion to regular Ajax. Time was of the essence if we were to fix our stalled Comet expansion before Ajax could neutralize our product advantage with a chlorinated copycat.

"What we need to do is re-sample parts of the country and increase our advertising weight to introductory levels in A counties where trial has been sub-par."

I went on to say that we had screwed up the introduction by mailing samples at the wrong time. Comet had developed a very efficient two-ounce sample can that could be delivered by third class U.S. Mail. The problem was that we scheduled the Comet introduction into very large markets in the month of

October and then mailed our samples smack in the middle of the Christmas rush. The samples were heavy, and they overloaded mailmen who just couldn't handle them. So, they dumped them by the thousands in garbage cans, on the doorsteps of apartment buildings and. of course, in large dumpsters. In other words, our samples never reached an unknown number of consumers where the concentration of porcelain sinks was greatest. That meant markets like New York, Philadelphia and Chicago where Ajax had most of its business.

Meanwhile, perhaps Ajax, aware of our sampling trouble, had doubled its advertising weight in A counties in an effort to make it even more difficult for Comet to obtain trial. As a result, Comet was grossly underweight in media in its most important cleanser markets. These markets were all the more important because stainless steel was replacing porcelain as the material of choice for kitchen sinks in new homes, largely in suburban areas away from A counties.

"Our leaders understood that the business runs best on the basis of trust and well-trained managers, supported by but not controlled by excessive structure or bureaucracy."

Howard looked at Bill and said, "How much is this going to cost?" Bill looked at me, because he didn't know yet either. I said, "It will only cost $7 million. With that, we can resample and restore our introductory advertising weight in all problem markets, mostly in A counties." That was a lot of money in 1956. It was like $70 million today.

Howard didn't blink an eye. He said to Bill, "Can we take it through the Administrative Committee on Tuesday?" Bill said yes, and the plan was approved. No, that was not the usual way you did things at P&G. You wrote memos. You prepared minutes. You obtained approvals from both the line and staff, and there were always lots of questions to answer. But, we did it with a gesture of Howard's hand.

I remember that I left his office thinking, "If this is an example of P&G bureaucracy, I'm all for it." Then I remembered that Howard had been one of the original Brand Managers, so he would have known instantly whether I knew my business or not. I also realized our leaders understood that the business runs best on the basis of trust in well-trained managers, supported by, but not controlled by excessive structure or bureaucracy. Further, all brands, all parts of the business should be run with a common sense of urgency.

John Pepper

I think that's a great story. If I may, I would like to move to Europe. One of the most significant things in the Company's history that happened was when you came to Europe in 1975 and began to Europeanize and eventually globalize our business by bringing together all the functions: Product Development, Manufacturing and Buying. This was a difficult thing to do, because the fiefdoms that existed country by country were powerful and resistant to changes that limited their freedom to alter their products independent of the rest of Europe.

Ed Artzt | Two major game-changing events preceded my 1975 arrival in Europe, and they set the table for what I was able to do. The first event was the elimination of duties on products shipped across borders in countries within the European Common Market. This meant that formula variations on a given brand could not be contained or prevented from going everywhere in Europe. This created an obvious need for Europroducts and the simplification they would bring.

The second event was the 1974 oil shock. OPEC, in protest against Western support of Israel's war with Egypt, quadrupled the price of oil from $3 per barrel to $12 per barrel virtually over-night. Everything related to oil went up in price, from electricity to petrochemicals to gasoline and motor oil. Europe was plunged into recession, and by the time I showed up in Brussels, all of our businesses in Europe were in profit trouble. Our profit for fiscal 1974-75 dropped by something like 64% percent versus the previous year.

Once again, enter Howard Morgens. Howard had stepped down as CEO in 1974, but he never abandoned his efforts to eliminate excess bureaucracy in the Company. Shortly after my arrival in Brussels, Howard made a victory lap through Inter-national and we got to spend some time together. He wasn't all that interested in digging into our ailing business. That was now Ed Harness's headache. But he did want to talk about the bureaucracy that he felt was afflicting P&G's Product Develop-ment performance in Europe.

I still remember Howard's words. He said, "I hope you recognize that we have this logjam in Product Research, and they don't seem to be able to move on anything. Everybody's got his own ideas about how much work was needed or how to change the product or how long it would take." He was talking about the Business Managers as well as the Product people.

He added, "The last time I was over here, I asked when are we going to get this new liquid laundry product, and everybody said the same thing — we're waiting for ETC — the European Technical Center in Brussels. We're waiting for ETC — that's the kind of thinking that led me to create Miami Valley. Nobody should be able to blame a lack of action on the need to wait for something that wasn't ready."

Howard liked to sing, and he said, "It's like everyone here is sitting around singing, 'We are waiting for the Robert E. Lee'." I adopted that as my theme song whenever it fit the situation. Nobody wanted to be identified with that song. It signified bureaucracy and inaction.

The first order of business in moving toward Europeanizing

**Wahib
Zaki**

Gordon
Brunner

our brands was to get stronger leadership at the top of Product
Development. It certainly appeared to me that as bureaucratic as
the U.S. operation was, it was much simpler than what we had in
Europe, and so I drew almost entirely upon my experience in the
Soap Business in Cincinnati to reach out to Bill Gurganus and
Ed Harness for help from the U.S.

We wound up getting the best of the best. Wahib Zaki, who had
been on assignment in the U.S., was transferred back to Brussels
as head of Product Development for Europe. We also brought
in Gordon Brunner from the U.S. business. Gordon and I had a
history of working together in the Food Division. I knew that he
would be an excellent successor to Zaki, when Wahib would be
summoned back to Cincinnati to succeed Harry Tecklenburg as

head of the entire P&G Product Research organization.

With Wahib in place, we consolidated two Product Development departments into one. They had been created to support Europe's two geographic Divisions. But, having two separate organizations working in the same house on the same product categories was a bad idea. It was largely responsible for the unproductive duplication of effort that gave us a plethora of different products, which we sold within Europe under the same brand name. For example, there were seven Dash products and five Ariel products clogging the system and slowing efforts to make our European products better everywhere.

By simplifying our products, we were also able to Europeanize our manufacturing organization. We started this effort with a detergent plant in every major country. Within a few years, we had reduced the number of factories producing laundry brands by half. As a result, we were able to produce more volume at less cost per case, and we were moving faster to test and expand business-building product initiatives.

John Pepper

We also had quite a bit of internal animosity between countries that worked against cooperation or teamwork across borders in Europe. I always remember when General Managers from eight or nine countries were called together about two months after I came to Europe. It was one of those sessions when we were asked to see how we felt about one another. It was a shocker. The Germans would say they thought the British were a bunch of weak debaters. The British would say the Germans were just Teutonic. Nobody respected the French or Italians. These were people talking about P&G people. It was one era when we lived as far apart from one another as you can imagine. Clearly, this was a tough set of attitudes that preceded our organization changes.

Ed Artzt | Yes. It's a good reminder that Europe is not a nation. National stereotypes will always influence attempts to establish unity among nations.

We also had other issues that needed to be addressed in order to establish a durable Eurostrategy. One was the misguided perception that there were barriers to individual career growth beyond the borders of one's home country. The other was the lack of employee identity with the parent company. For starters, Americans were P&G shareholders; Europeans were mostly not.

On the first issue, we were a multi-national company without a multi-national management. This was a function of history. P&G entered the UK in 1930, and was the main source of management talent to run European subsidiaries that were mostly created after WWII. For example, we entered France in 1954, Italy in 1956 and Germany in 1960. To their credit, the American and British expats did a good job of recruiting local talent for these new subsidiaries. But, by 1975, when I got to Europe, we had a bunch of 40-something local managers who were ready for promotion, but were blocked by former British expats, who had become permanent employees of their subsidiaries and weren't going anywhere until retirement.

To make matters worse, headhunters were coming after our people, and one of their main arguments was, "P&G will never promote a local national to lead a European subsidiary." "P&G is worried that you will put allegiance to your country ahead of allegiance to P&G." I could see that we were headed for the eventual loss of our best European talent if we didn't unblock this additional logjam. So, I decided to set a goal of having a local national manager at the top of each European subsidiary within a year, and while it took a little while longer in some cases, that's what we did.

The promotions, as I recall, were Helmut Fischer and Wolfgang

Berndt to General Managers in Germany, Claude Meyer as GM in France and Sandro Baldini as GM in Italy. Other important promotions included Harold Einsmann of Germany to General Manager of Benelux, Jürgen Hintz from Germany to Country Manager of Holland, Jorge Montoya, a Peruvian national from Advertising Manager to General Manager of Spain, and he was backed up by Eduardo Baeza, a Spanish local who later became GM of Spain. So in one fell swoop, we protected many of our best young managers and dispelled the misinformation about P&G's unwillingness to put locals in charge of their own country's subsidiaries. Some of the moves worked out, some didn't, but four of the managers advanced to bigger jobs as officers of the parent company later in their careers.

The other issue was a lack of identity with the parent company, which can be illustrated by a flap over the tradition of the P&G annual Christmas basket.

John Pepper

I remember that one as I was on the receiving end in Italy. In the U.S., we had something called a Christmas basket. It was the Company's Christmas message to employees. In Cincinnati, it usually contained a Christmas ham, dessert, cheese, crackers, a box of Cracker Jack and one or two P&G products. It could vary by location, but it was always the fixings for a family meal.

Now Ed comes over and asks his staff head, Tom Collins, "What's in the Christmas basket?" The answer was "five bottles of booze." That's it. By the time it got to me, Ed had cut the booze to one bottle. When I presented the news to my Management Committee, I was met with a chill. "We have to have two bottles. One Spumante, and one red. Anything less and the organization would revolt." I went back to Ed to plead for two, and he said yes. But these were the kinds of things that people ran into.

Ed Artzt

A small incident, but a meaningful example of the different ways that employees related to P&G in Europe. It all came to my attention at lunch one day when we were asked to stand for a moment of silence to recognize an employee who had died in an accident at our Belgian factory. I asked what happened. They said, "He was drinking at lunch, and he fell off a scaffold. Belgians drank wine with lunch, so we sell it in the plant cafeteria." I said, "Why don't we stop doing that?" They gave me the same "employee revolt" reply that you got in Italy, John, and that's when I brought up the Christmas basket question with Tom Collins.

He not only confirmed that the contents of our ETC Christmas basket were five bottles of booze, but also that authority to decide the contents had been delegated to our ETC Works Council as a gesture of capitulation over their responsibilities. I said something like, "That's the dumbest thing since our Founders decided to add live turkeys to the Christmas basket, only to have the turkeys escape on their way home and terrorize downtown Cincinnati."

That was different. Turkeys were on the point. Five bottles of booze missed the point. I said, look, there's a simple way of dealing with this. The P&G Christmas basket is a gift from Procter & Gamble to its employees — a reminder that we are a company of families. It is not a gift from the Works Council to themselves. The Christmas card from the Company has my name on it. Why the hell would we turn such a sensitive matter over to the Works Council, who now considers it an entitlement? These are the kinds of mistakes that make the Company look foolish to its overseas employees.

John Pepper

I would like to return to Japan, a critical subject in the Company's history. You were a big part of it, as were Durk Jager and John Smale. Could you tell the story of what got us into it, the tension over staying? I was totally removed from it.

| Ed Artzt | Some of this will repeat what I said earlier. I was on the Board from 1972-1975; after that I moved to Brussels for five years to run Europe. We entered Japan in 1973, so I was directly involved in Board meetings only in the early years in Japan. |

Early in 1972, Ed Shutt, then Division Manager for Asia, was charged with exploring entry strategies for a P&G assault on the Japanese market. Japan's merger laws required that foreign companies could not buy Japanese firms. They could only partner with them. Therefore, Ed surfaced with a proposal to enter by forming a joint venture in the laundry detergent business with a company called Nippon Sunhome. Shutt had reasoned that we had no P&G people who had worked in Japan; therefore, local knowledge would be critical to success. He was right about that, but he was wrong about the proposed Japanese partner, a virtually bankrupt business with weak brands and even weaker management.

The whole Japanese entry process was plagued by either unforeseen circumstances or by self-inflicted wounds.

1. **Gurganus**

    Bill Gurganus, then the boss of P&G International, had vigorously and vocally opposed our entering Japan and refused to be responsible for running it if we went ahead. Morgens made the decision to proceed anyway, explaining to the Board that P&G needed to learn how to build a business in Japan if we were to become a major international company.

    Gurganus, on the other hand, had a strongly held belief which was based on many years of international experience with mergers, acquisitions and partnerships. He used to tell me, "Don't acquire weak companies. Buy or partner with strong companies with healthy businesses. If they lack certain expertise, make sure that ours is suited to their market."

Bill felt so strongly that P&G would fail in Japan, given the uniquely hostile business environment and the lack of a decent partnership option, that he simply refused to have anything to do with it.

2. Competition

A large part of Gurganus' objection traced to the fact that Shutt's search for a Joint Venture partner had included talks with Kao and Lion, the two largest detergent competitors in Japan. God only knows how much we told them about our plans for entering Japan, but they both turned us down. It was immediately clear to Bill and our people that they considered us enemy invaders, not potential partners, and would react accordingly. They did.

Their strategy was predictable. Since P&G always entered large countries with locally manufactured laundry detergents, they elected to price their core laundry brands at or just slightly above their cost. That way they would be in compliance with Japanese antitrust laws, and since our costs were much higher than theirs, we would either have to premium price or bleed red ink. We elected to bleed until the 1974 oil shock, and then we hemorrhaged. Meanwhile, Kao and Lion were both able to finance their detergent defense with other core profit centers, including feminine hygiene, shampoos and oral care.

3. Loss of Management Continuity

I have already mentioned P&G's Management changes at the top of the Company. Those happened in 1974, the year after we entered Japan. Ed Harness became CEO, replacing Howard Morgens. Brad Butler took what would have been Bill Gurganus' role at the top of the Japan venture. This was in addition to Butler's role as P&G's Chief Staff Officer. No doubt that the duo of Harness and Butler could have dealt with any mess in Japan, but their new Corporate responsibilities required their full attention elsewhere. They had bigger fish to fry, at least until Japan went into the tank.

4. **P&G Staffing**

Meanwhile, Ed Shutt proceeded to fill the key P&G jobs in Japan with average performers. They were competent, experienced veterans from the U.S. and Europe, but this was not a job for average performers. First and foremost, it would require adaptive changes in U.S. products.

A successful entry in Japan would also require a much deeper understanding of Japanese habits, practices and lifestyle. It would also require major adaptive changes in pricing, sales and advertising strategy and execution, and we weren't making them. The greatest self-inflicted wound by P&G came from the belief that, "What has worked for P&G in the U.S. is what we will do in Japan." For the first few years, P&G followed that strategy out the window, and so we made some costly mistakes.

5. **The 1974 Oil Shock**

When OPEC increased oil prices from $3 to $12 per barrel in 1974, the consequences in Japan were quite severe. Overnight, there were widespread price increases for energy, fuel and raw materials, triggering a consumer recession in Japan. The sudden price inflation also gave Kao and Lion an opportunity to put more pressure on P&G's detergent business. They simply dragged their feet on pricing up so that consumers would load up on their brands.

6. **Sales Strategies**

Japan's unique pyramid distribution system was a well-known

barrier to entry for many foreign companies. Brad Butler, perhaps the smartest sales mind at P&G, had concluded that we had little chance of succeeding by just working within the old system. So, he decided to attack it U.S.-style with promotions that called for deep-cut featuring in Japan's large chain stores. That, too, proved to be a costly misstep, because it threatened the profit structure of the wholesale network.

Japan's retail trade was dominated by small stores; there were 1.7 million outlets in total with 60% of them having no more than two employees. The heart of the system was the network of 335,000 wholesalers, consisting of large wholesalers selling to smaller jobbers/wholesalers who had their own warehouses and did the selling and delivering of goods to retailers. A package of detergent was usually handled two to three times before reaching store shelves, and each of the wholesale handlers marked up the price to cover their profit margins.

Supermarket chain stores, on the other hand, were supplied directly from their own warehouses at lower costs, but chain supermarket development in Japan had gone slowly because of space limitations and government interference. They only accounted for about 20% of the turnover in Japan in the mid '70s.

P&G's dilemma was that most of the wholesalers were under contract with either Kao or Lion, and P&G was distributing through a relatively weak group of less-effective handlers. Further, in those wholesalers who sold P&G detergent along with Kao and Lion, we were considered second-fiddle suppliers, and we were unable to cultivate the kind of close personal relationships that were characteristic of the Japanese distribution system.

7. **Cheer**

It's remarkable that Cheer lasted as long as it did in Japan. Its self-inflicted wounds were so severe. Here are the things that mattered most.

I.   The U.S. All Temperature Cheer approach was a laughter to Japanese consumers. They were washing clothes in cold water, either tap water or leftover bath water, and we were telling them to sort their clothes in separate piles for hot, warm and cold water. Students of doing business in Japan called that ethnocentric orientation, a fatal form of tunnel vision.

II. The U.S. sales strategy of promoting deep-cut price featuring in chain stores caused widespread resentment among the wholesale distributors in Japan. I believe that Cheer never got more than 60% net distribution in Japan due to our alienation of the layered wholesale/jobber trade. Its highest market share had been 13%, but by 1983, it was 9% and declining.

Jack Nedell, P&G's General Manager in Japan, later wrote a book titled, "Around The World in 80 Years." Jack overlooked a lot, but his firsthand descriptions of the travails of our early years in Japan are worth reading.

III. We failed to back up Cheer with a second brand that would put pressure on one of Kao's core profit centers in order to disrupt their detergent pricing strategy. We just did not have the brands to do that until several years later, when we developed products designed for Japan, principally Japanese versions of Ariel, Always, Pantene and Ultra-Thin Pampers.

8. **Pampers**

Unfortunately our second entry, Pampers, fared no better than Cheer, even though it had no serious disposable diaper competition until Unicharm introduced Moonies in 1981. This gave us a four-year head start with what proved to be the wrong product. During that time, we had only converted about 10% of Japan's diaper changes to Pampers, and we had an 84% share of that 10%. Moonies cut Pampers to 45% in its first two years and, when Kao introduced Merries with "breathable sheet" in 1983, the Pampers business hit the wall. How did all of that happen?

I. Once again, we based the whole entry plan on the assumption that successful U.S. products should be accepted by consumers just as well in foreign markets. So, since we had no manufacturing capacity in Japan and no product research underway to create a different and better product for Japan, we charged ahead to import U.S. Pampers. At that time, U.S. Pampers consisted of a layer of tissue wadding sandwiched between a rayon top sheet and a polyethylene back sheet.

II. The U.S. product was bulky, stuffy while dry and it leaked when wet — but it was still better than the cloth diapering system for many mothers. However, we were sitting ducks for Unicharm's introduction of thin diapers with a super absorbent polymer gel filling and for Kao's superior sheet technology. We were behind the Japanese in diaper technology until 1986 when the Ultra-Thin Pampers product was introduced globally. By then, we were already producing Pampers in Japan at our new Akashi Plant, but I don't recall the timing of our conversion to the Ultra-Thin product there, or whether it was the U.S. or European version. The European product was better.

III. We also failed to respond creatively to the fact that diapering habits were much different in Japan than in the
U.S. or Europe. Japanese mothers carried their babies
around in backpacks which quickly alerted them to the
need to change diapers.

So, the average diaper change frequency in Japan was 14
times per day versus six times in the U.S. and Europe. As
a result, Pampers, which were designed for heavy loading, were considered to be too bulky and too expensive.
Mothers also disliked the stuffiness and leakage that they
experienced with Pampers, and they worried that, as a
result, Pampers would cause diaper rash.

IV. Another self-inflicted wound was caused by poor management of the hospital sampling program. Sampling
new mothers at birth was critical to Pampers' success
because the diaper market turned over every two years.
Pampers had to be continuously reintroduced to new
mothers and returning mothers who had been out of
the market for some time. The key to that reintroduction process was the hospital sampling program, which
consisted of supplying hospitals with Pampers for their
nurseries and sample packs of newborn-size Pampers for
the mothers to take home.

The problem — the hospital staffs were taking delivery
of the samples, but most maternity nurses were not
using them or giving them to new mothers when they
left the hospital. We later determined that there was a
long-standing negative bias against disposable diapers
which coincided with the shortcomings of our U.S.
product. We, in turn, made matters worse by failing to
monitor the sampling program, and therefore, did not
take steps to fix it until Durk Jager arrived in the early

'80s. We had a selling job to do on Japan's maternity room nurses and hospital staffs, and we weren't doing it.

V.   The need to import Pampers into Japan and pay duties made the brand expensive during the pre-Akashi years. This of course was unavoidable, but it was part of the assortment of negatives that hindered Pampers ability to displace cloth diapering and create a significant market for disposable diapers.

Shane Meeker | Wow.

Rob Garver | How did Procter & Gamble release Pampers in Japan without knowing all of those things? I mean, Procter market tests everything.

Ed Artzt | I think we have to step back and look at more than just Pampers. I am sure there are several theories. I have mine.

Once the Company decided in 1972 to enter Japan, we did so in too much of a hurry. We were ill-prepared. We had grossly underestimated the technical expertise, creativity and mobility of Japanese competitors. Kao's boss for example, Dr. Yoshiro Maruta, was a superb chemical engineer, who had studied P&G and other U.S. companies for years. However, until we tried to become his partner, we hardly knew who he was.

We also had no people who had lived or worked in Japan. And for some reason, we were willing to overlook the experience of dozens of U.S. companies that had failed in Japan. In fact, we ignored our own similar experience with Tide in Europe and Latin America. Gurganus, of course, knew all of this, but Howard Morgens must have wanted to get Japan underway before he retired in 1974, and when Howard wanted to move, we moved.

Let me say this another way.

We failed to embrace the Harness doctrine, which was: "If you enter a new market (or country) against entrenched competition, you must do two things. Number one, bring a better product that cannot be easily matched and two, focus on beating the number one competitor, where most of your business must come from. He will certainly be focused on you."

During our first seven or eight years in Japan, we relied on Cheer, a parity product, wrongly marketed, and on Pampers, the wrong product for Japan, poorly marketed. Further, we were not able to attack the competition's most vulnerable profit centers until we introduced Japanese Ariel, Whisper and Ultra-Thin Pampers, all in the 1980s and Pantene in the '90s. Had we waited for those brands, we might have been more successful. Impossible to predict, but I believe we were just not ready to enter Japan when we did.

John Pepper

I am trying to understand the timing of this. When did you take over Japan from Brad Butler? Was it after your promotion in 1980? When did Durk Jager come in?

Ed Artzt

I became head of the International Business in 1980 and took over Japan from Brad Butler in mid-1982. John Smale had wanted me to first digest Bill Gurganus' countries before tackling Japan. Those included all of the business under Samih Sherif, including the Middle East, Hong Kong, China, Greece and all the export markets. In addition to Sherif's operations, there was Mexico and the rest of Latin America.

Durk Jager came after I took on Japan in 1982. He was transferred from his job as the Country Manager in Austria to Advertising Manager in Japan, reporting to our General Manager, Russell Marsden. Marsden was UK-trained with an advertising

"If you enter a new market (or country) against entrenched competition, you must do two things. Number one, bring a better product that cannot be easily matched and two, focus on beating the number one competitor."

	background. He was Vice President of Southern Europe at the time. Russ sadly suffered a stroke and was unable to return to his job. I don't remember which year, but Durk was ready to step up, so he became General Manager of Japan; it must have been 1984 or 1985 by then.
John Pepper	How difficult was the Board? How challenging? Did they believe that we had to be in Japan?
Ed Artzt	They were helpful. They were supportive of our being in Japan, but they were concerned that we had made so many mistakes. I had been a member of the Board for three years before the Company entered Japan. So, I was a party to the original deliberations

and a known quantity when I returned from Europe. I definitely felt that the Board was willing to give John Smale and me a shot at turning Japan around, but at that point, pulling the plug was definitely still a live option if we didn't succeed.

As I recall, Japan became profitable for the first time in 1987. By then, we had corrected many of the internal problems and marketing mistakes, and had launched Ariel (1986) and Whisper (1986) and had converted Pampers to the Ultra product globally (1986). Cheer converted to the compact form, but the brand didn't survive.

Shane Meeker

I saw an article about a speech you gave called, "The Future of Advertising." I'd love to hear some of the insights you had at the time that caused you to choose that subject.

Durk
Jager

I was invited to be the keynote speaker at the 4A's Convention, which was a big event in the advertising industry — with some 400 attendees, including the CEOs of all the important agencies. The 4A's chose the subject, thinking that the talk would be about all the good things that we saw in the industry's pipeline for the future. Also, because P&G was the number one advertiser in the U.S., I would be a logical choice to deliver the message.

Only that's not the message I delivered. I felt that the industry needed to wake up to the fact that the economic foundation of commissionable television advertising was under assault by subscription and pay-per-view companies who would be offering advertising-free entertainment. They, the agencies, should not only be concerned, they should be organizing to protect the future availability of advertising-sponsored television programming. Without it, we would all be in trouble.

I enlisted the help of Bob Herbold, our Advertising Vice President, and he wound up doing most of the work. I had the basic outline in my mind, which Bob also shared.

I was glad to accept the 4A's invitation, because I knew from our contacts with our P&G agencies that they were struggling with the dilemma of what to do about the threat to the future of their business. Pay-per-view was around the corner. Advertising-free subscriptions were coming as well — all of which meant that consumer-paid programming and movies may eventually replace sponsor-paid programming.

Despite the concern, nobody was leading an effort to organize the industry to deal with this threat. To my dismay, the apparent solutions being pursued consisted of running away from the problem, rather than trying to solve it. For example:

1. Some of the largest agencies, like Y&R, were attempting to

replace lost commissionable ad revenue by adding services like public relations, sales promotion and business consulting. This strategy did nothing for their core business of creating, producing and purchasing advertising.

2. Even more worrisome was the fact that most of the major U.S. agencies were for sale. The owners and shareholders were focused on cashing out and were in the process of being acquired by European companies.

This was not a healthy environment for protecting a threatened industry. I felt that we needed to inject a large dose of reality into the talk, so we videotaped interviews with the top executives who were leading the assault on advertising-sponsored television, which, by the way, accounted for 80% of P&G's U.S. advertising spending back in 1994.

We were able to line up a number of the key players, including Sumner Redstone of Viacom, John Malone of TCI, Larry Tisch of CBS, Tom Murphy of Capital City/ABC, Jerry Levin of Time-Warner and Barry Diller of QVC. We used a Q&A format, similar to "60 Minutes", with Bob or me interviewing people off camera. The message came through loud and clear. The network chiefs sounded complacent and wanted to reassure the agencies. All the other guys sounded the alarm.

They each predicted that the consumer would have multiple programming choices, both with and without sponsor-paid advertising. John Malone created the biggest shock wave when he predicted that his consumer-paid venture was imminent. He said, "Our timetable for making services available is to have our terrestrial facilities in the U.S. completed by the end of 1996, so that would be 2 ½ years from now."

Sumner Redstone challenged the agencies to get back into program

content. He said, "The race is for content, and content is king."
The agencies used to control most of the original programs, and
the advertisers would sponsor them. Subscription channels like
HBO and Netflix have long since replaced the ad agencies as
content providers.

The speech attracted a great deal of media coverage. It was
described as a wake-up call to the advertising industry, and it has
been revisited by the press several times since.

In 2004, Jim Stengel, then P&G's Chief Marketing Officer,
gave the keynote speech at the same 4A's Convention that I had
addressed 10 years earlier. He did a very good job of comparing
what I had warned the industry about in 1994 versus what had
actually happened since. I would suggest that Jim's speech be
attached as an addendum to my oral history.

John Pepper	Very interesting. Frankly, agencies have been very slow to get reinvolved in owning or producing content. P&G is back into it, but the agencies are mostly not. Instead, the internet has been developed into a major advertising medium for both the agencies and sponsors alike.
	I was struck by another talk you gave in 1993 called, "Stop the Hate," addressing racism in the workplace. That was 26 years ago. Do you remember the speech? It was passionate.
Ed Artzt	I remember it very well. The Martin Luther King Jr. Foundation in Atlanta sponsored an annual Salute to Greatness fundraising dinner every year, and they invite somebody from the corporate sector to give the keynote speech. I was on the Delta Air Line Board at the time and so was the former Mayor of Atlanta, Andy Young. We sat next to each other at Delta Board meetings and had become good friends.

I believe that Andy recommended me to the King people when they were looking for a keynote speaker. So I said, sure, I'll do it and went back to Cincinnati thinking, what am I going to say? The audience will know 10 times more than I do about this subject. It will be comprised of many famous African American community leaders and celebrities from all over the country.

Fortunately, P&G had hired Vernon Jordan as a consultant to guide the Company during the affirmative action era. Vernon was a lawyer who had been a close friend and supporter of Dr. Martin Luther King Jr. He was sure to be present at the same event in Atlanta. I decided to seek his advice. I told Vernon that I wanted to talk about racism in the workplace and asked him, "What do you think I should do to get ready for that?" He said, "Talk to your people."

So, we gathered together a group of about 20 young African American P&G employees in a conference room in the Cincinnati headquarters. After briefing them on my King speech assignment, I told them that I wanted them to tell me what it's like to be a Black employee in a predominately white company.

"P&G always tries to do the right thing, but often struggles to understand the problem it's trying to fix. Racism in the workplace is one of those problems that we need to understand a lot better, and I want you to open your hearts and minds and tell me what you have experienced here. I want the message I deliver in Atlanta to be informative for our employees, to the supporters at the MLK Foundation and to the business community as a whole."

The responses from our employees were amazingly frank and quite helpful. As we went around the table, each person said pretty much the same things, backed up by their own personal experience within P&G.

The point they all emphasized was that the racism that they lived with at P&G was not overt. It was "subtle, debilitating and largely unrecognized." They described their feelings with the term "pain threshold" which was the added burden of having one's opinion discounted, or failing to receive deserved credit or recognition, having to work to a different standard than one's peers and seldom receiving the benefit of the doubt in close-call situations.

As you know, John, those interviews became the heart of my talk, which was very well received by the audience in Atlanta. The one comment I remember most was, "Somebody finally gets it." Unfortunately, this type of problem requires cultural change — teaching children to respect and not look down upon others because of their race or origin. Anti-discrimination laws and policies alone won't do it.

| John Pepper | Sounds like our employees opened up very quickly in that room. |
| Ed Artzt | Nobody had invited them to share their opinions on that subject before. |

"Each of my assignments provided lessons for reapplication. Each required that I try to understand what had caused the problems in the first place."

John Pepper	One other thing you did that I believe was important around that time was your recognition of the LGBT community. Our P&G LGBT group wanted to change our diversity code to recognize sexual orientation as a factor that should not in any way discriminate against anyone. The change in the code had been held up in the bureaucracy for some time, but when it got to you, as the story goes, you signed it in about five seconds and said, "Why not, of course, people are people."
Ed Artzt	Frankly, I don't remember the incident very well. I knew it had been an issue, and I had some personal contacts with the subject both inside and outside the Company. For example, I was aware that Dick Cheney, one of our Directors, later Vice President of the United States, had a gay daughter, and Rob Portman, a classmate of my son's, had a gay son. I had been close with both the Cheney and Portman families for years. I was also well aware of the fact that Susan Arnold had a lesbian partner, and they had two children. It doesn't surprise me, therefore, that I was receptive to that change in our Company code regarding the LGBT community.
John Pepper	You came away from so many assignments with important lessons to learn. Were there any of these lessons that you were able to reapply?
Ed Artzt	Every assignment I had provided lessons for re-application. Each assignment presented different problems. More importantly, each required that I try to understand what caused the problems in the first place. Those same kinds of problem/solution situations could be found in all parts of the business. That's why we created P&G College to record and disseminate the lessons to our people. For me personally, our experience, both good and bad, with geographic expansion in Paper was re-applicable to our ex-

pansion of Folger's into the East Coast five years later. Samih
Sherif's export markets were full of re-applicable lessons. The
most important one for me was the fact that healthy, growing,
established brands could be successfully expanded as new
brands into new geography, while stagnant or declining established brands usually flopped. This was an important foundation principle in guiding our international expansion strategy
in the '80s and '90s.

During my Paper years, we proved that there could be important
incremental synergy from combining demonstrable product
improvements with packaging and advertising upgrades to help
signal the change to consumers. We ship-tested CPF Charmin
blind and not much happened. In another market, we added
poly packaging for the first time and got a good share bump over
CPF alone. In a third area, we added both the poly and Whipple
announcement advertising copy, and together, I recall, they delivered about a 35% increase in Charmin's share and shipments.
That execution was in contrast to many instances where we
simply flagged product improvements with a patch saying "new
and improved" and did much the same in advertising. Think of
the difference in the product presentation of Tide Pods with that
of Tide Packets years ago.

An important lesson I took away from my Coffee days was my
personal experience with commuting to Kansas City. It was:
"Don't allow your people to live and work away from their families for any great length of time."

When I was appointed acting General Manager of Coffee in
Kansas City, it was supposed to be for about six weeks or until
Ed Korpe, the previous GM, recovered from surgery and could
return to that job. Unfortunately, he did not recover, and I wound
up commuting to work for a year. The drill was three days in
Kansas City one week and five days the next. Then back home

on the weekends, plus two days a month to attend Administrative Committee meetings. I was told by my boss, Bill Snow, that after my replacement could be appointed, he would retire, and I would replace him as Group Vice President over Coffee and Food. So I had plenty of incentive to feel good about the Coffee assignment.

"We proved that there could be important incremental synergy from combining demonstrable product improvements with packaging and advertising upgrades that signaled a change to consumers."

However, I also discovered that continuous commuting had downsides for families that should be avoided whenever possible. In that situation, you quickly become something of a stranger in your own home. Waiting for you each weekend was all the bad news you did not get during the week. Bills for the house and car, for example. The kids, especially teenagers, are busy with their own weekend activities usually not involving parents.

When I got to Europe, I discovered that some of our British Managers were keeping their families in the UK while working in permanent jobs in Brussels. This had its origins in a company decision in the early '70s to localize the compensation of International Managers who were no longer on temporary assignments of two years or less; International Managers were not always required to move their families, but for permanent assignments, P&G insisted on it. Our policy was simply, if you want to accept a permanent position outside your home country, you need to bring your family with you.

John Pepper   It doesn't work long term to break up the family.

Ed Artzt   Well, aside from being bad for families, it set a dangerous precedent. Our European Technical Center in Brussels was staffed with people recruited from many countries. We needed to be consistent on the matter of separating families, especially at the top, where such examples are usually set. Said another way, we wanted our European headquarters to be a community of families and not a terminal for employee commuters.

John Pepper   Looking back over the course of your career, what are the words of advice that are as valid today as they were 25 years ago? In other words, what are the most important things that haven't changed?

"P&G principles are timeless; while the Company changes with the times, the principles do not."

| Ed Artzt | Well, of course, P&G principles are timeless, and while the Company changes with the times, the principles do not. P&G is certainly more socially progressive than it was 25 years ago. |

When it comes to remembering advice, I believe that the most valuable words for me had to do with the criteria for selecting executives from within the Company. There were three principles that stand out in my memory:

1. Morgens used to say, "Get right at the top. If you're not right at the top, nothing is right." He meant the top of any discrete part of the Company — a brand, a subsidiary, a department or an acquisition. If you conclude that you have a wrong manager at the top, it is your job to replace him.

2. Whenever you acquire a business or a company, put your own manager in charge. Otherwise, everything will happen too slowly. This also came to me from my talks with Howard Morgens.

3. One that John Smale preached and practiced was, "Seek out Managers who know what to do, and not just how to do it. These are the people who think strategically and are most likely to select the right options for the Company to pursue." John was a brilliant strategist, and he would quickly spot that gift, or the absence of it, in others. He also insisted that our performance evaluations of individuals cover strategic thinking as a measurable strength or weakness. This would be based on the individual's awareness and definition of opportunities and problems, definition of options to pursue and ingenuity of thinking.

| John Pepper | Anything else on the question of what has not changed that should not change? |

"Seek out Managers who know what to do, not just how to do it." Ed Artzt quoting John Smale.

Ed Artzt	I think that consumer tastes are bound to change, but I also think that consumer loyalty will always be there.
John Pepper	You talk a lot about consumer loyalty. You gave talks about how you keep this loyalty to consumers and not lose it. You gave huge emphasis to the idea that you should never give consumers a product reason to switch from your brand. Focus on that as a commitment.
Ed Artzt	Yes, consumer loyalty to every brand has to be renewed. Otherwise, the consumer can be devastatingly fickle. That's why I have always stressed that rule: "If you have the market leader in a category, never give the consumer a product reason to switch away from your brand." We did not follow that rule on Pampers (Shape) and Tide (Liquid, Oxy).

As a result, we were slow to embrace the concept of mega-brands, but I think we have learned our lesson. New technology was always a constant in the evolution of consumer brands, and consumer loyalty to competitors has always been an obstacle that P&G overcame with most of its big successes. I hope we have fully embraced the idea that, "When something you want or need in a laundry detergent comes along, you won't have to switch away from Tide or Ariel to get it. We'll bring it to you in products like Tide with Oxy or Tide Pods, etc." |

The advent of mega-brands was greatly facilitated by the internet, which enabled brands to offer new variants without having to displace existing shelf space in retail stores. Secondary brands have benefited too, and it simply means that consumer brand loyalty is easier for them to penetrate and harder for P&G to protect.

Another factor in the evolution of consumer loyalty is each generation's need for its own identity. I believe it is embedded in the human DNA that each generation must be different from the one before. It's why teenagers look different, wear different clothing, dance and sing to different music and speak a different language. In other words, figuratively speaking, nobody wants to drive their parents' Buick. It wouldn't be cool.

Brands that endure retain their relevance to the constituencies of several generations. They successfully accommodate the necessity of re-inventing their products to meet contemporary needs. They do that without abandoning their aging customer base. It seems to me that among others, P&G's Old Spice, Crest and Tide have done that well. Olay, over the years, has not. Neither has Gillette.

The Gillette management had long followed the successful strategy of reinventing the premium-priced top of its line, while continuing to offer past models as long as they were in demand. But a new generation of young, bearded men were vulnerable to the online shave club assault, and like new mothers, they did not inherit loyalty to their parent's brand. Theirs had to be captured, and Gillette responded too slowly to avoid a major loss of market share, despite having superior products at the top of its line.

Consumer loyalty is an organic condition. It can thrive for decades and then vanish in a few years or less. It is most vulnerable to the toxic effects of obsolescence. P&G, by itself, was one of the earliest victims of brand obsolescence when we lost our candle

business and our laundry fat soap business to new inventions. That experience was one of the reasons why we have always spent so much money on upstream R&D. We tried to never forget that consumer loyalty to new technologies can trump loyalties to old brands that have become obsolete.

A different form of obsolescence can afflict whole industries. Look at what the internet plus the development of fulfillment technologies by Amazon are doing to the retail shopping world. Loyalties to retailers are moving online.

John Pepper   One of the things that is most significant to the period of the '90s and 2000s was the very intentional approach you brought to the expansion of brands globally. I would be in

"If you have the market leader in a category, never give the consumer a product reason to switch away from your brand."

all the meetings, but we would never leave a meeting room without a plan to introduce Pantene and Always. It wasn't happenstance, and it resulted in those brands becoming worldwide leaders by large measure versus the number two brands in their categories.

Ed Artzt   John Smale and I agreed at the outset of our working relationship in 1980 that globalization of our business would be a primary growth strategy for the Company and not just a goal. It would require major changes in the way we did things because globalization was not just a decision to sell our products internationally. It was a way of planning and operating which begins with a worldwide strategic planning process and carries through to technology deployment, product supply investment, marketing execution — all the way through to delivering the product to the consumer. A fundamental objective was to avoid preemption of our technologies and ideas by fast-following competitors who would to take advantage of the timing gaps in our rollout plans.

We agreed at that time that the International organization needed to be involved in the product work for new brands as well as product upgrades that were candidates for expansion in the United States. We needed to do the work on product tailoring early rather than wait until the U.S. product was all we had validated for foreign expansion.

"*Globalization was not just a decision to sell our products internationally, it was a way of planning and operating which begins with a worldwide strategic planning process and carries through to technology deployment, product supply investment, marketing execution — all the way to delivering the products to the consumer.*"

In order to facilitate this, we created globalization teams with members from all of the functions and several major countries. These teams were responsible for bringing a complete plan to the Company for approval before exposing a new product to competition. They were also responsible for incorporating foreign test marketing in their plans. These teams would not displace our traditional organizational approach to managing foreign subsidiaries. We would still need strong local management of the profitability of P&G's brands in each country. The new globalization strategy would be limited initially to new brands like Always and Pantene and game-changing technologies like Ultra-Thin Pampers, concentrated high-density detergents and 2-in1 shampoos.

Finally, the Company would need to determine the capital and marketing resources required to support our expansion plans so that the bottom line impacts could be reflected in our overall company profit forecast.

Clearly, my five years in Europe were the catalyst for my conviction regarding globalization of the business. We had been

badly hurt by our own failure to pre-plan the sequencing of the expansions of new or improved brands in Europe. As a result, far too much time had elapsed between our first entry and the rest, because we were usually beaten to market by fast-following competitors. In other words, we were the second or third brand in with products we had invented.

Three brands clearly demonstrated the price we had paid for slow European expansion of our brands. Lenor was the first P&G fabric softener in Germany, and it was the market leader with a share in the mid-'70s. It was the second, third or even the fourth brand introduced into the rest of Europe, where it never came close to matching Lenor's leadership or shares in Germany.

The same pattern was repeated on Ariel and Mr. Clean. The longer we took, the worse we did, because Henkel, Unilever and Colgate were very nimble, fast followers. The problem that needed to be corrected was evident in our approach to strategic planning. There was too much dependence on local authority to tell the Company what brands each country wanted to introduce and when to introduce them. Moreover, Europe's key business centers lacked the product development staffing or capital funds to support fast European expansion. So, the local subs tended to favor incremental product upgrades that could be manufactured at their local factories.

The results of the strategic changes we made proved to be quite significant. Pampers, for example, had taken 10 years to expand into 78 countries, with 64% of its business outside the U.S. by 1991. Along the way, Pampers experienced many setbacks due to its late entries. Also, Pampers was impacted by both fast-followers and also fast-initiators, namely, Unicharm and Kimberly-Clark. Against that background, we were able to get Ultra-Thin Pampers diapers expanded in all of those markets in less than three years. Other examples include Pantene, where we entered 32 of the most important countries in just 10 months. Always/Whisper was introduced in 30 countries in just two years and achieved a 20 share before competitors could preempt our technology.

John Pepper   Right, and the benefit is crystal clear. The question in my mind is how hard was it for you to sell internally? This was a way different approach to the organization.

Ed Artzt   It wasn't too difficult. John Smale gave it his complete support. So did the Board. The key for me was communication and involvement. Had we not included our foreign managers on the global teams, we would have not been able to make the system work. Also, I made it a point to review our progress frequently because the results were so conclusive.

John Pepper   What was the most important factor, besides involvement of our international people, in the global strategy teams?

Ed Artzt   I believe it was the stretching timetables. P&G people like to be challenged by stretching goals, and they almost always meet them. Everyone knew that we needed to move faster. No pushback there. The question was, how fast? So, we said to the organization, "We're not going to start expanding a new brand or a major upgrade unless we can finish in an agreed-upon number

"The global teams can do the overall planning, but the countries must add the creative execution for each initiative."

of countries within two years." We met or beat those goals on both Always and Pantene.

The toughest hurdle for most stretch timetables was the need to commit capital for new capacity. Lead times were long and costs were high, so P&G usually committed in waves. We decided instead to do as much temporary contract manufacturing as we could. The premise was that it was better to risk loss of confidentiality than to manufacture in-house and be late to the market.

Another critical challenge was what I would call, "Marketing readiness." How do we best present a new or dramatically improved product to consumers in 20 or 30 countries all at once? We needed diverse test markets. Pantene was a classic example of how important marketing readiness was to the reinvention of this brand. Remember, Pantene went from a flop in the U.S. to a billion-dollar world market leader in record time due to the work of the globalization teams. Everything had to change, including the product, the packaging, the advertising and especially — the positioning.

Initially, nobody wanted to test market Pantene, but I eventually found willing participants in both Taiwan and France, I believe.

"Our promotion-from-within policy reflects the belief that we can train people to be better managers than anyone else can."

Test marketing confirmed that just incorporating 2-in1 product technology into the shampoo and presenting Pantene with advertising that promoted healthy hair supported by "Pro-V vitamins" was not enough. Two further changes were needed. The most important was to add a separate Pantene conditioner to the shampoo and market them together as a "treatment." The second was the healthy hair TV visualization created in Japan. The combination of all the changes was tested, and we were ready to go with a winner.

The Pantene success was similar to the way we used single-variable testing to combine components into our CPF Charmin expansion back in the 1960s. In that case, we ran single-variable tests with CPF tissue only, poly packaging only and Whipple advertising only. When we combined all three, the synergy effect literally catapulted the business to new highs.

I would like to wind up this topic by emphasizing the point that getting the marketing right was a key element of a successful global strategic plan. That means there must be active involvement of the local national subsidiaries in the process. The global teams can do the overall planning, but the countries must add the creative execution for each initiative, as well as the test market locations. It should also be recorded that other components, ranging from advertising to unique promotional activities like Always' premenstrual program, can synergize consumer response to new P&G products.

| John Pepper | I wanted to make sure that the talk you gave at the Harvard Business School and many other places on, *How to Be a Winning Manager* is captured here in these notes. One of the things that you talked about is what these students should be looking for in the company they join is that the company not only is good, strong and will teach them the business, but that the company will really care about their |

development. Maybe you can expand on that. I'd just like
that to be in the oral history; it is so important.

Ed Artzt | One of the things that I worried about most throughout my
career was whether P&G could continue to reinvent itself by
promoting from within. I have always believed that promotion
from within has great benefits for a company like ours, as long as
we are able to hire the best people right out of school. Entry-level
recruiting provides us with our lifeblood, and I had grown concerned that we were not doing it well enough.

Our promotion-from-within policy reflects the belief that we
can train people to be better managers than anyone else can.
P&G training has always been rich in discipline and in the skills
of communications. This has given the Company enormous
advantages in the ability of P&G people to work together across
functions and nationalities and to transfer from one part of the
Company or from one country to another.

When I wrote the *How to Be a Winning Manager* talk, I was
addressing future P&G recruits, and the section you mentioned
was an attempt to explain the advantage of working for a company where your boss would care about your development, not
just your performance. At P&G, everyone is responsible for
developing the people under them, because we are committed to
promoting from within.

The inspiration for this talk really came from an experience I
remember from my first attendance at a Cincinnati year-end
meeting in 1954. I was in one of the presentation meetings when
our Chairman, Neil McElroy, walked in and agreed to answer
questions. Someone asked him about the just-announced organization change which created separate operating divisions with
their own line and staff support. McElroy had a booming voice,
and I remembered he answered, "Organizations exist at P&G

"Recruiting has to be proactive, and Management including Senior Management, should be involved in it."

to provide the best framework for the development of people." Those words, and the message behind them, stayed with me throughout my career.

Nevertheless, I have always had misgivings about our ability to sustain our management excellence in all parts of the Company with the policy of promotion from within. It can be done if our recruiting succeeds in attracting the top people from the top schools. But it won't succeed if we lapse into a recruiting policy that mainly treats recruiting as a screening process. Recruiting has to be proactive, and management should be involved in it.

If you look at P&G's recruiting history over the decades, you will find that we were very successful during two periods of history when conditions in the job market favored us greatly. They were the Great Depression in the '30s and the years immediately following World War II — 1945-1947.

During those times, the Company saw the opportunity to stock up on the cream of the recruiting crop, because there would be far more candidates than jobs, especially fast-track career openings like ours.

During the Great Depression, from 1929-1932, we hired Neil

McElroy, Howard Morgens, Bill Snow, Rowell Chase and Jake Lingle. Gib Pleasants joined in 1934, and Ed Harness came in 1937. In any case, we scored a recruiting bonanza in the depths of the Depression because we were proactive at a time when almost nobody else was hiring. Howard Morgens explained it in one of his oral histories. He was asked why he chose to join Procter & Gamble. Howard said, "It was the only offer I had. It was the Great Depression. I didn't know anything about Procter & Gamble, but I needed to make some money. A year after I graduated from the Harvard Business School, 70% of my classmates still had no job." The point here is that the Company chose to be proactive at the right time, and it paid off with the hiring of three decades of future management.

"If you want to hire the best and the brightest, the keys are proactivity and management participation. You go after them; you don't wait for them to come to you."

After the end of World War II, the nation's universities and graduate schools loaded up with veterans under the GI Bill who would shortly flood the market with qualified candidates.

I don't have a complete list, but there was a brief period after the war when we hired Bill Gurganus, Pete Link, Jack Hanley and the returning Ed Harness, who had worked for P&G pre-war. Here again, the Company seized a temporary opportunity to recruit a prime crop of future leaders. I'm sure we did the same in the technical divisions as well. We've always been able to hire outstanding people, but even in the best of recruiting years, we have had to go after them proactively. I hope we are still doing that.

Bear in mind that the policy of promotion from within was not always supported by recruiting; originally, it simply supported family succession and enabled family control of the P&G partnership. That worked for three generations from 1837-1930 when RR Deupree became the first non-family President of the Company. One of Deupree's first executive decisions was to establish pro-active entry-level recruiting in the midst of the Depression. Four years earlier, Deupree hired one of the Company's first chemical engineers, Vic Mills.

As you might expect, however, decades of economic growth and prosperity brought new competition for the best entry-level young people everywhere. Competition increased within our own industries, but it largely arose from new "in" career paths, such as Management Consulting, Investment Banking, Silicon Valley and the Information Industry — not to mention the Sciences and Engineering industries as well. The new stiffer competition offered higher salaries, preferred locations, attractive perks and more initial responsibility. Meanwhile, we had stayed with the practice of depending on HR staff to turn up qualified candidates. They did a good job of screening, but an important element was missing — contact with P&G managers on campus.

The battle for talent in the 80's and 90's was fierce, and as we reviewed our internal talent resources, I became concerned that we weren't winning it. Our acceptance rate had been declining, and that's why we decided to put together the more aggressive recruiting approach, involving the creation of university recruiting teams and the active involvement of managers from all levels and all Company disciplines.

John Pepper

Well, it's a very systematic approach to organization development. Getting teams together, going to campuses and measuring management performance in terms of hiring results. Line managers were doing the recruiting for the first time — very much like P&G College. The linkage between recruiting and P&G College training is not surprising. It was getting line management into the business of developing the organization.

Ed Artzt

As I said earlier, if you want to hire the best and the brightest, the keys are proactivity and management participation. You go after them; you don't wait for them to come to you. Also, you use real-life line management to demonstrate that P&G really cares about the development of its employees. To be frank, I borrowed a page from the college coaching profession, where the best teams usually come from the best recruiters year in and year out, beginning with the personal involvement of the coaches. Think Alabama in football or Duke in basketball, where the coaches spend two-thirds of each year recruiting new high school talent and consistently come up with the number one rated team in the country.

Rob Garver

When did you start having regular contact with John Smale?

Ed Artzt

Regular contact started in 1980, when he became CEO, and I became the head of International, reporting to John. I had met John before, but I believe it was just in P&G social situations or Company events.

Rob Garver

When you think of him in general, what are your main memories of him as a person and manager?

Ed Artzt
My main memory of John is of our friendship; we were close. We traveled together. We visited each other's homes in Florida and Wyoming. We fished together; we had fun. So, mostly my favorite memories of John Smale were of times away from the business. We enjoyed sharing thoughts, and we were very open with each other. It was something that developed over time. I don't think that he was just being a good boss. We were relaxed around each other, and the chemistry was always good.

At the same time, we had a very clear understanding of our business relationship. He was my boss, and I never had any trouble with that. What did I think of John as a manager? He was superb, profound and inspirational. He was considerate and respectful with the people around him, but he was unmistakably clear and precise when giving orders or directions. He was an outstanding strategic thinker partly because he was an ardent student of the business. John's ability to dig and probe into the details of a subject enabled him to see things that others had missed. It was a great strength.

John and I were quite different in personality and management style, but we thought alike. Maybe it was our P&G training, but on important issues, we almost always came out in the same direction — not on the same next steps, but on the direction. If it looked like we were not agreeing on something, John would always try to work it out, and on matters of judgment, he would often defer to me or my subordinates.

Rob Garver
It doesn't surprise me that you thought alike. John had made some comments about how people learned and how things were passed on within P&G, even though they hadn't been written down. Instead, they were handed down in conversation in offices, and they were all consistent in their description of P&G's character.

Ed Artzt | Yes, as I explained earlier, the ritual of the daily lunch in the old Gwynne Building headquarters feeds right back to that, but the Company outgrew the practicality of having mandatory daily lunch discussions. While the Executive Dining Room was moved to our new headquarters in 1964, the tradition eventually ended with the retirements of Deupree, McElroy and Morgens.

However, a large measure of the "campfire" communication ritual was embodied in P&G's weekly Administrative Committee meetings, which were held every Tuesday morning at 10 a.m. in the Cincinnati headquarters. Attendance consisted of all the Vice Presidents and Division Heads and above, including visiting International officers.

The underlying purpose of the Administrative Committee was command and control. It was not a decision-function, but rather, it was a formal gathering of the Company's executives to report and record all action that had been approved by the Chief Executive or his delegated subordinates. Normally, decisions requiring Administrative Committee recording could be implemented before reporting them in the Administrative Committee, but the delay was seldom longer than a week.

The Company rules were very precise in defining which actions by the management required Administrative Committee authorizations. They included the establishment of new brands, major changes in package design, product test marketing, capital appropriations above a specific threshold, price changes and annual budgets and marketing appropriations. The Administrative Committee was the command center for the very strict discipline that P&G exercised over all parts of the business. But it required the CEO to get involved in everything of material substance, and by the time the Company was divisionalized and had increased its international presence, the Administrative Committee process had become something of a bottleneck.

Despite the load of formal business that had to be processed by the Administrative Committee, the meetings were the ideal forum for the CEO and other senior officers to comment on the principles involved or the lessons learned with each action. Frequently, the Division heads would play that role in the description of the action that they were reporting. I had discussed these learning experiences in Administrative Committee many times as a Division or Group Vice President. It was there that I developed much of my thinking about P&G College.

Quite often, the events that demonstrated the consistency of the character of Procter & Gamble were embodied in the explanation of why we were doing or not doing certain things, not just what we were doing. The value of the forum can't be overestimated.

Inevitably, global expansion of the organization outgrew the practicality of weekly meetings of management in Cincinnati, and they were eventually replaced with much larger, less frequent gatherings in various parts of the world. I don't know what the Company uses today for command and control of authorizations, but I am sure they perform the recording function.

What may have been lost are the vehicles for passing along Company lore and learning to the new generations of P&G Managers. That is why I still believe in the need for P&G College or its contemporary equivalent.

Rob Garver

John Smale said that all institutions like P&G have more than just bricks and mortar they have a soul, and they represent a character. Did you see that in him — this idea that P&G was really kind of a living thing that needed to be guided and grown?

Ed Artzt

Yes, definitely. We all felt that way, and it may very well have been kindled by RR Deupree. He was frequently quoted as attributing organic qualities to P&G's organization. Deupree said something like the following during the depths of the Great Depression, "You can take away our factories, even our products, and all of our material assets, but if our people survive, they would surely recreate P&G as we know it." He was expressing the belief that the soul of P&G was embedded in the hearts and minds of our people, and that gives them the regenerative capacity to survive calamity, while other companies may not.

John also had a special vision when it came to explaining the soul of the Company. He could see things better than most, and he could explain them better. He took his responsibility for communicating the inner strength of the Company very seriously, but he did not follow it out the window.

John loved to ask certain P&G Managers, "What business would you say we are in?" And when they would say, "Consumer products or meeting consumer needs," John would say, "No. We're in the business of making money." Then he would whack the errant manager for failing to deliver his profit forecast. That was not his answer for everybody, but it was an effective way of getting his point across to managers who were focused on the wrong things and not delivering satisfactory profit to the Company.

As you might guess, when the press queried John with the usual questioning, "What kind of company is P&G?" John would say, "We're a product company. We invent and market products that make people's lives better." John was aware that the press liked to attribute our success to our advertising and promotion spending, and John wanted to tell both our P&G organization and the financial community that the Company's greatest strength was its Research and Development excellence, not the money it spends. And by the way, he believed that 100% — a conviction he developed during his years on Crest.

Of course, John also knew that we had been under attack by the FTC in the 1960s, and were forced to divest the Clorox business. The FTC had argued that P&G's marketing muscle might give it the potential to restrain competition in any new business it entered. That was a terrible abomination of the anti-monopoly powers of the Federal Government. But each of us, thereafter, was ever conscious of the purpose and strengths of P&G, first and foremost in terms of our R&D inventiveness — which was absolutely true.

Rob Garver   All right, let's talk about some of the more specific things that happened in the Company, like Richardson-Vicks. P&G didn't have a lot of time to make the decision to acquire Richardson-Vicks because you were brought in as a white knight. John Smale had been looking at them for about a decade since he once worked there, but I don't know whether you were really prepared as a company to do the kind of due diligence that you normally do. Do you recall the negotiations at all?

Ed Artzt   I was not in those conversations. I was running P&G's International business then.

John Pepper   Yes, it was 1985. I was working in Europe and also was not involved.

Rob Garver   Well, could you talk a little bit about the impact of that particular acquisition on the future of the Company.

Ed Artzt   Well, the impact came from the part of the Company we didn't buy it for, beauty care. Think Pantene and Olay. We valued Richardson-Vicks mostly for the platform it would give us in the OTC cough/cold business. The Vicks franchise had two bell cow brands, Vicks VapoRub, a household staple internationally since the 1918 flu epidemic, and Nyquil, an important player in the nighttime cold/flu relief segment, mostly in the United States.

But the real superstars of the Vicks acquisition were the beauty care brands, Pantene and Olay. P&G paid $1.2 billion for Richardson-Vicks when we bought it in 1985. Their sales had been $1.2 billion with earnings of $72 million in that year. Olay was well established and very much a strategic target, as well, but it was not growing.

By 2015, the last years for which I have estimates of sales, Pantene had reached $3.8 billion and Olay $2.5 billion. Not bad when you consider that Pantene was a mere $25 million in sales in 1985. The story of how we turned Pantene into a blockbuster is worth telling. Olay was not well managed in recent years, but that's another story.

Pantene had been a stepchild at Richardson-Vicks. It was originally sold to them by Hoffman-La Roche, and they had run it into the ground. It had developed a small but loyal following as a direct application hair restorer sold and applied in barbershops and beauty salons. Richardson-Vicks also marketed a Pantene men's hair tonic, which also had built a small loyal following in France, but nowhere else.

In 1986, P&G's U.S. Company took the lead in attempting to turn Pantene into a successful shampoo brand, based on the 2-in1 technology that had already achieved modest success in the U.S. in Pert Plus. International ignored Pantene, choosing instead to incorporate the 2-in1 technology in a shampoo under the Vidal Sassoon brand, which was another piece of the RVI acquisition. Results there were modest to unsatisfactory.

The U.S. effort was pretty much a bust. They had chosen to stick with a Richardson-Vicks-developed gold-cap bottle that looked more like a bug spray container, and they launched it with one of our biggest advertising flops, "Don't hate me for being beautiful," starring Steven Segal's wife, Kelly LeBrock.

Meanwhile, we had formed a joint venture with Agrolimen, a Spanish diaper manufacturer headquartered in Barcelona, Spain, and I was invited to attend a very elaborate celebration of that event with the Carulla family at the Barcelona Opera House. I was the senior member of the P&G delegation, so I was seated

"The real superstars of the Vicks acquisition were the beauty care brands, Pantene and Olay."

directly across from Luis Carulla, the founder and principle own-er of our partner. Luis Carulla spoke not one word of English. He had been a hero in the struggle for Catalonian independence from Spain, so nobody even spoke Spanish, just Catalan. But we both had interpreters. It was 1989, four years after we purchased Richardson-Vicks, and obtained Pantene.

As background, P&G International did not have a good record with cosmetic shampoos, but we did have the leading global brand in Head and Shoulders. So, we were definitely looking for a way to crack that market with our 2-in1 product technology. However, I was in Barcelona to celebrate baby diapers, not sham-poos. Then, the first miracle occurred. Luis Carulla was gestur-ing wildly and messing up his bushy head of hair, and virtually shouting at me in Catalan.

I asked his interpreter, "What is he saying?" He was saying, "Look at my hair! I've been using the Pantene treatment every day for 35 years, look how bushy it is." He made a hell of a mess out of his hair just to give me the message that this stuff works, and he's living proof. I didn't know what to think, but initially, I just chalked it up to one of those interesting coincidences. Here we have a very smart man saying that he owes his bushy hair to Pantene. At least he didn't say, "Don't hate me for being beautiful."

Then, miracle two landed on my doorstep, or the other way around. I was in Buenos Aires, Argentina, on Company business, and I needed a haircut. So, I went to the barbershop in the hotel, and while I'm getting my hair cut, I noticed that the guy sitting next to me was getting something rubbed into his hair by the barber. I asked him what he was doing and he said, "Pantene. It makes hair grow." I said to myself, someone is sending me a message, this can't be coincidence, we had better do something about this.

So I went back to Cincinnati and looked up the history of Pantene at Hoffman LaRoche. It turned out that they had solid evidence that the Panterol in Pantene was effective at repairing damaged hair. That was short of making hair grow. But hair growth would not be necessary to support the claim, "Hair so healthy it shines."

I started talking Pantene with our managers. I said, "Who would be interested in test marketing a whole new approach on Pantene using the Pert Plus 2-in1 technology?" Two countries volunteered, France and Taiwan. Taiwan, however, put it all together, similar to Charmin CPF in the '60s.

John Pepper   Yes. James Wey was the Country Manager in Taiwan.

Ed Artzt   Right. James had embraced a technique that was developed in International called, "Search and reapply," and he was anxious to reapply an incredibly riveting television visualization developed by our advertising agency in Japan. He also reached for some Japanese packaging design work on the Pantene shampoo and treatment conditioner. The advertising campaign, "Hair So Healthy it Shines," was created by Grey in New York in 1990. Thanks to James Wey, the Pantene products, the advertising campaign and Japanese visualization were combined and sold as a treatment system. And the brand took off like a rocket. I can remember being concerned that competition might discover the success we had in Taiwan and expand it before we did. But, we succeeded in getting the Taiwan Pantene combination expanded into 32 countries in about 10 months. By 1994, Pantene was the number one shampoo brand in the world.

Rob Garver

Did Smale figure into the Pantene decisions or was that the kind of decision that didn't get to that level?

Ed Artzt

I am sure he did. There were important product decisions, and there were investment appropriations that had to be reported in the Administrative Committee. I know he was very supportive since we had agreed early on that the key to turning Japan into a profitable business would be the successful marketing of new brands like Pantene and Always/Whisper in categories which were the most profitable for Kao. Meanwhile, we were bleeding red ink in our core laundry detergent business, and we concluded that something dramatic had to be done about it.

Some Kao background is important here. Kao's President Yoshiro Maruta was a legendary leader of Japan's post war economic reconstruction. He was a chemical engineer and an experienced plant manager. When he became President in 1971, he firmly established the Company principle that product research and development was to be the focus of the Kao Company — and indeed it was.

Kao's strategy for defending itself against P&G in Japan had two major segments — new innovative products in P&G's two core categories, detergents and diapers. The second segment was continuous pricing of its laundry detergents at cost — their cost, which was well below ours. Their product research effort resulted in the 1983 introduction of Merries diapers with tapes and a breathable top sheet, and the 1987 introduction of Attack high-density compact laundry detergent. We had products in development that would eventually counter Merries and Attack, namely Pampers Ultra and Compact Ariel, but we were still under heavy profit pressure from Kao's pricing policy, which the rest of the industry was following.

Both Durk Jager and I believed that the industry had colluded in an effort to convince us that we could never make money in Japan, and, therefore, like many other American companies, we should leave. We also suspected that we might have been the targets of reprisal by Japanese detergent companies for our aggressive promotional behavior in chain accounts. That had angered our competitors as well as the wholesale trade.

In any case, we were in a no-win situation, and I came to the conclusion that we needed to blast our way out and hopefully convince the industry, and especially Kao, that we were in Japan to stay. So I went to John Smale and said, "We might have to do something wild in order to break this logjam." John said, "Let's not do it too wild. We have to explain it to the Board." I said, "Well, I think we need to make their pricing behavior more costly for them than it is for us, and the only way to do that is with a price decline on Cheer that they have to then match — like 50% for three months." John said, "You mean a promotion?" I said, "No, a price decline. It's not just for the chains. We figured it would cost us $500,000, but it will cost Kao $15 million to match us. I hope that will get across the message that they are not going to price us out of Japan."

Meanwhile, we expected to regain some lost distribution, build some share and help repair our damaged relationships with the wholesale trade. John said, "OK, but you are going to explain all of this to the Board when we meet in a couple of weeks — not me."

Well, it worked, but not exactly in the way we had anticipated.

Yoshio Maruta, Kao's President, was also the President of Japan's Soap and Detergent Association, a group of industry competitors that had turned P&G down for membership. When Maruta learned about the pricing action, he sent a letter to the Association membership, which somehow got into the hands of the U.S Embassy's Commercial Attaché in Tokyo. The text of the letter escapes me, but it went something like this, "The interlopers from the United States have struck again. They are trying to get into this country, and we must use all available means to stop them." There was more, but the entire letter implicated the industry in illegally colluding to restrain competition.

The U.S. Attaché presented the Maruta letter to Japan's FTC, triggering an investigation into the detergent industry's pricing practices. At the same time, the Japanese press joined in decrying the humiliation that Maruta had brought down on himself, his company and the industry, reminding everyone that Japan Inc. was indeed a reality. Shortly thereafter, Maruta retired at the age of 73. We had won the day in our effort to eliminate the industry's predatory pricing against Cheer, but Kao's new brands, Merries diapers and Attack detergent, eventually proved to be far more threatening to P&G's survival than their pricing defense.

Rob Garver   Was that the turning point for P&G?

Ed Artzt   Yes, it was. I think we operated in the black the year after that. However, no one event or brand turned the business around in Japan. It was the combination of people and product moves, which included Pampers Ultra, Compact Ariel, Whisper and Pantene, plus Joy dishwashing liquid and the acquisition of SKII. These initiatives, the leadership of Durk Jager and the pricing event, together, turned Japan from a chronic problem market into a major profit contributor for P&G.

| John Pepper | Do you remember any disagreements between you and John Smale that couldn't be resolved. If so, how did they get resolved? |

Ed Artzt — I'm sure there were some, but I can't remember any that were important enough to recount here. Of course, John was responsible for protecting the total Company profit forecast, and that meant saying no from time to time to requests for short-term spending increases that would reduce earnings for the year. When the CEO says, "No, we can't afford to take the hit," you don't argue. You go back and try to make the spending increase profit neutral or you just withdraw to fight another day.

John Pepper — I'm sure there must have been situations like that.

Ed Artzt — Let me add a story that goes back to one of my first meetings with John after he was promoted to CEO, and I was promoted to the head of International. I said to John, "Let's see if we agree on a strategy for the International Business for the next few years. We have so many options that it would be very helpful to have a mutual understanding of what we're trying to do so that we're not fighting in the trenches over each proposal."

Without hesitation, John said, "We're a company that supplies products to men and women all over the world. But, we've been far too slow in getting them out there for them to use. I'd like you to help me make us a truly global company."

My response was measured, but very positive. I remember telling him, "I'm sure we can do it if we remember all the lessons we've learned in the past 20 years about opening new countries and expanding established brands as new brands, and staffing new subsidiaries and joint ventures. We don't want to create any more European Tides or Japans." I also told John that my understanding of a global business strategy would mean investing in developing countries with lower standards of living than P&G historically required — countries like China, India, Russia and the rest of Eastern Europe. We would also need to seek entry opportunities in South Korea, Brazil, Argentina and Chile. Those countries had underdeveloped, growing economies, but volatile political histories.

John kept nodding affirmatively and finally said something like, "Keep us out of trouble, but those countries are where all the people are that we need to reach." So, the decision was made in that one first meeting. Globalize our geographic footprint, our major brands, and most importantly, our organization. Soon after that discussion with John, I presented our strategic vision to the P&G Board and obtained their blessing, too. We were off to a good start.

The next step was to work out a master plan, which called for giving priority to Asia, Eastern Europe and Latin America. At the same time, we sketched out an organization plan that would incorporate new territories under our existing International Divisions, and draw upon the management talent with the most experience in setting up new businesses. We had a lot of talent outside of the United States, not just in the management, but in all of the disciplines. However, the U.S. organization had far more resources to draw on for a global product strategy. So, when we blended together all the talent and all of the U.S. resources, it gave us a much more focused organization for executing a global business strategy.

There were many key players involved, especially Samih Sherif, who had headed the export and special operations division. Samih had led the Company's entry into Saudi Arabia, Egypt and the rest of the Middle East. He was our international expert on joint ventures and partnerships. Samih also played the key role in forming our first joint venture in China.

In addition, Herbert Schmitz was one of the key managers for Eastern Europe startups, including Russia, and Jorge Montoya, who was the Vice President of the Latin American Division, was the man in charge of new ventures there.

At the same time we were forming our management teams, we started hiring college graduates from Russia, China, Poland and other target countries for P&G training even before we had made our initial expansion investment in their home countries. These people were able to combine their local knowledge with P&G methods and were extremely valuable in directing local marketing of our brands. They were vitally important participants in our globalization movement and the prime recruiters for additional local talent in their home countries.

I don't want to get into all of the details of P&G globalization here. That could fill a book in fact, John, you filled a book on just P&G in Russia. I read somewhere that during the 1980s, P&G increased the number of countries with operations on the ground from 22 to 46 and that number continued to go up in the 1990s.

Rob Garver

Two things on globalization. Why was Smale focused on becoming global, and can you make the distinction for me between international and global?

Ed Artzt

Well, one is just organizational. International is every business outside the United States. Global includes the United States, and, therefore redefines the responsibility for bringing products to market that can be sold throughout the world. If you go back to the early days on Tide, P&G was still basically an American company that also exported its products overseas — even in later years. After we recognized the need for product tailoring geographically, we did so with regional technical centers in Europe and Asia and not with a global focus on deploying technology, or controlling the number of product variations necessary to successfully market a brand worldwide. It's a fact that the greater the number of regional groups, the more proliferation you have, and the slower you move.

John Smale knew that, and he was focused on globalization because he wanted more customers for the business. But, he also wanted the product development and brand marketing functions to be conducted on a worldwide basis. Remember, he said that we had been moving too slowly to capitalize on our inventive resources.

John Pepper

I just want to underscore the point Ed is making. Until about 1980, when Ed took over International and John Smale made the Global commitment, International and the U.S. were like two different planets. The whole idea of integrated R&D, product supply, purchasing and marketing was not part of our history. Also, you still have to understand the local market differences. Otherwise, globalization is not going to work. That's why we continued to run the day-to-day business with strong local subsidiaries.

Rob Garver

Did that play into the structural changes that took place in the 1980s — category management, product supply and so forth.

Ed Artzt

Those changes certainly helped. Product supply was created to make purchasing, manufacturing and distribution a seamless process, not a collection of independent P&G suppliers of goods and services from one department to another. Without the product supply model, globalization would not have been manageable across continents. The same conclusion applies to category management, since we had more than one brand in several categories, requiring the same coordinated planning regarding product deployment decisions, priorities and capital requirements.

Rob Garver	Back in the '80s did you and John Smale talk a lot about organization structure?
Ed Artzt	More about people than structure. We were committed to keeping the framework of our geographic structure, but we needed to create additional Divisions in Asia and Europe, for example. We also agreed that we wanted to avoid adding layers to deal with the workload effects of global expansion. In fact, John and I had both grown up in heavily layered parts of P&G, and we both felt that delayering was an important imperative if we were to become more nimble and more efficient as a company.

John had many areas of focus during his tenure, but his particular interest was financial. He believed that too many of our managers, particularly in International, were insufficiently concerned about low profitability as long as their business was growing in volume and market share. That partly accounts for his habit of reminding people that "making money" was P&G's main business.

John had served on the J.P. Morgan Board for a few years, and he had been impressed there with how much more literate their people were about the financial measurements of business performance.

Or course, their business was primarily about managing and investing money. Still, with the exception of Manufacturing, Product Development and Corporate Finance, John was dissatisfied with the P&G organization's attention to improving profitability. Manufacturing and Product Development had a system for creating, funding and recognizing Savings Projects, which had proved to be enormously successful at reducing costs. A Savings Project required a payout of three years or less, and the benefit usually went straight to the bottom line, or occasionally made other Savings Projects possible.

The Brand and Country Management organizations at P&G

were somewhat insulated from the multitude of financial activities that could affect the profitability of their businesses. Those groups did not receive EBITDA data — and for good reason. We had always employed a profit management system based on Bogey or target P&As. The P&A for each brand and country was computed based on direct cost, assigned R&D and Administrative overheads, and actual marketing expense.

P&G top management had always wanted the people in its profit centers to worry about what they could control, and they wanted to establish comparability across the Company's businesses. That is why the profit centers were never given EBITDA numbers. The effects of Corporate decisions for tax management, interest costs or Corporate investment decisions could inflate or deflate the bottom line of each business. It was a good system, but the profit centers and the brands always tended to believe that they had more control over volume and share than they did over profitability. John wanted to change that misconception, and I personally supported that effort 100%.

Rob Garver

How did you go about it?

Ed Artzt

Several ways. First, by creating new profit transparency with the addition of "Return on Investment" as a pillar of our accounting system. I am not sure of the year though; it might have been in the '90s. I also recall that we made changes in our bonus system to make it more reliant on profit performance. Finally, and probably most importantly, by constant crusading by both John and me personally, on the road, in the office and in our Company meetings.

John had his opening line, "What business are we in." I had my Harry's Carpet anecdote. I would say, "Have you ever heard of Harry's Carpet?" The answer would be no, and I would follow with, "Harry is the proprietor of Harry's Carpet Stores in Cincinnati. In his advertising, Harry always ends with the line, 'I don't care about making money. I just love to sell carpet.' You remind me of Harry, only Harry does make money because he actually hates to sell carpet at a loss."

Rob Garver When did you find out that John Smale was going to retire and you would replace him?

Ed Artzt I was not forewarned of that decision until it happened. I was returning to Cincinnati from a business trip when John called me on the Company plane. He said, "Ed, I need to see you tonight. I hear you are coming into Lunken Airport. Can I meet you there at 8 p.m. for a quick conversation?" When I arrived, we went straight to the Chief Pilot's office, closed the door and sat down. He said, "I've decided to retire, and the Board has decided to have you replace me." I was stunned, but I stayed calm.

The only preceding discussion of the subject of succession took place some months earlier. I don't remember what triggered it, but I made it clear to John that he could count on me to continue working until he retired from P&G. I told him, "When you go, that's when I'll go." I was assuming that he would continue on to 65, but he apparently decided that he did not want that to happen.

That night in the airport, John said, "You know, I'm doing this for your sake, so that you can be the CEO of the Company and have a run at it. I know if I stay on for a couple of years, which I could do, it might be too late for you." John and I were three years apart in age. When John stepped down, I was only 59, so he thought I could have a good run and make a difference. John was 62 at the time, and that had been par for the course for retiring CEOs. Morgens retired at 62, Deupree and Harness retired at 63 and I eventually retired at 65. Fortunately, I was healthy and had lots of energy to take the top job at 59. But John had made quite a concession, for which I remain very grateful.

How to Become a Winning Manager

March 2, 1988

At that time, Mr. Artzt was Vice Chairman of Procter & Gamble and President of P&G International.

Mr. Artzt addressed students at the The Wharton School, Lauder Institute of Management & International Studies, University of Pennsylvania, Philadelphia. He subsequently delivered this speech on many other campuses as well.

One of the things that I did in preparing for this presentation was conduct a little small-base research with a few MBA students to get some ideas on what you'd like to have me talk about.

It was interesting to me that the most frequently suggested topics for today somehow involved a personal career path. What does it take to get ahead? What are the requirements for business leadership in the future? And, it doesn't surprise me as spring approaches, that many of you are starting to think very seriously about your careers in business, and your personal development in whatever line of work you select, either here or internationally.

I'm going to try to give you some things to think about — based on my own personal experience and my own convictions, as well as the broad experience that our Company has had in developing people who win in management.

It's a fact that there are winners and losers in management and most are not born that way. You learn how to win. If you don't, you lose.

I think it is a safe assumption that everyone here this afternoon has a high level of intelligence, native ability and personal ambition. Some of you will make it to the top of your professions. Some of you won't. All of you will need to grow. All of you will need to correct weaknesses and develop skills that have yet to be fully tested in your work or school experiences to date.

I want to try to give you some insights today that may help you plan your own personal development, so that you will go as far in your business careers as your talent and willingness to work can take you.

Winning in management requires an exceptional combination of attitude, skills and personal character. These are the three things I'm going to talk about. There are others. You can slice this subject lots of ways. We could talk about leadership, entrepreneurship, brilliance and street smarts.

But I want to focus on attitude, skills and personal character, because these are things that develop you, and you can work on them every day and in every job you hold.

Attitude

Let's start with attitude, and I want to talk about only two aspects of personal attitude. One is professionalism. The other is winning as a way of life. They are closely related.

Everything, good or bad, in a business career starts with attitude. What you want (and what you're willing to give up to get it) is a function of the attitude you bring to your work. What do you want? To be successful? To be rich? To have power? To run your own business? Good. There's nothing wrong with that. But, let's think together about a more actionable goal — to become professional. More than that — to become a master professional in whatever line of work you choose.

Professionalism

Do you know the main difference between an amateur and a professional? Between an average professional and a master professional? It's very simple. It's mastery of the fundamentals. And, that's what you must do to win in management. You must master the fundamentals of the business you're in, of the functions you perform and of the process of managing people. If you don't do that, you'll eventually become a journeyman, or journeywoman, and the brilliance you once had will surely tarnish.

Mastering the fundamentals of any profession, be it in the arts, sports or business, requires great sacrifice, endless repetition and a constant search for the best way to do things. All of the great master professionals understood that. Beethoven, Mozart, Segovia, Michelangelo understood it. Jack Nicklaus and Vince Lombardi understood it. In business, Sam Walton of Walmart understands it. Iacocca does, and so did the late Gus Levy, who learned arbitrage in the mail room at Goldman Sachs, and went on to become one of the great master professionals of investment banking.

But these men were geniuses. So were a lot of geniuses you never heard of. These geniuses worked their tails off to become master professionals.

The point I want to make here is that a professional in search of mastery brings an attitude to his work that no sacrifice is too great and no experience or grunt work too menial, if it helps achieve mastery of the fundamentals. If you want to become a winning manager, I urge you to embrace that attitude with all your might.

Winning

What about winning as a way of life? What has that to do with attitude and management? The answer is everything. The winning manager has trained his mind to win against benchmarks, as well as against opponents, in all phases of life. What benchmarks? All kinds. In business, if you have a quota, beat it. If you have a budget, underspend it. If you have a financial target, exceed it. If you have a deadline, get in under it. If you promise 10, deliver 15. If you bring that attitude to your work, a constant striving to beat the benchmark, you will find yourself developing the essential tools of competitive advantage that you'll need to win in the marketplace.

My point here is that learning to win in this very tough, competitive world is not something that you do only when it counts. You have to try to make it part of your attitude toward life, certainly a part of your attitude toward work.

Skills

Let's move on to skills. What are the skills to master at the professional level if one is to become a winning manager in today's business world? There isn't time to cover them all, so I'll skip the functional skills, like financial or marketing, or analytical, or linguistic and cultural skills on the assumption that you're either learning them here or will ask me about them later.

I want to talk about personal skills. I want to talk about three — communication, prioritization, and strategic thinking — all of them require skills that you can develop over time across a broad spectrum of competence, ranging from bland mediocrity to black belt mastery.

Communication

Let's start with communication — one of the most underdeveloped skills in the arsenal of young professionals entering business today. If you want to run the show someday and run it well, you had better learn to think, write and speak, in that order — clearly, forcefully, concisely and to the point.

You can learn how to do that. At P&G, we teach people to do that. We think it expands a manager's capacity enormously if he communicates well. We also think that an organization has a much better chance of beating the competition if people really understand what they're saying to each other, and occasionally, understand what the boss is saying to the organization.

Clarity of written communication is just as important. I recall one time many years ago when a young man in my Brand Group, relatively new with the Company, wrote a two-page memorandum proposing that our Company develop and market our first liquid household cleaner. At that time, we dominated the market with Spic & Span powder. The proposal was forceful, persuasive and articulate. It made its points clearly and with appropriate understatement. It was approved.

A day later, Neil McElroy, the Chairman of the Board, appeared in the darkness of my doorway (there were no windows in my office then). He had the memo with him.

"Can this young man really think this well?" he asked. "Yes," I said. "That's his thinking." "Well then, why don't we promote him?" McElroy asked. We did, and he did well, and I received a strong commendation for my role in training him to communicate his thinking so well. I've never forgotten that illustration of the power of good communication in the management process. This young fellow who had been with the Company just a short time had, with the power of two pages of written communication, moved the Company to take a major initiative in a new business. We all felt like winners that day, believe me.

You can learn to communicate at a professional level. There are books to read, courses to take, good rules to follow. But above all, try to work in an environment that gives you some disciplined training. Remember, you cannot always present and sell your ideas face-to-face, especially if you're in France, and your boss is in another country, or if you're consulting and your clients need to expose your thinking to others in their hierarchy. Communi-

"The ability to first distinguish and then focus energy on those few issues that would produce a real impact was a primary quality among the best performers."

cation is a skill that will quickly separate the winners from the losers on most management ladders.

Setting Priorities

Prioritization — I've chosen this skill as the second of three because of its importance as a building block in developing your skill as a strategic thinker.

In a business sense, prioritization is working on the right things, in the right order, with the right amount of energy and focus. Early on in school, we learned the value of working on the important things first, and putting the trivial and fun things aside, and in their proper order. At least we try to learn that, and in the process, have to deal with our own human instinct to procrastinate. Later on in business life, we face much the same challenge, only we are busier. Personal prioritization is a matter of developing good habits. Having those good habits can be terribly important to your developing strong prioritization skills in the management of people, organizations and strategies.

One of the leading consulting firms did a major study in 1984 called *Identifying and Developing Exceptional Managers*. One of the key points in that study was that there were four performance factors with the highest correlation with exceptional management performance. They were initiative, decision-making efficiency, leadership potential and willingness to take appropriate risks. In the discussion of decision-making efficiency, the report highlighted this point about prioritization:

> *"The ability to first distinguish and then focus energy on those few issues that would produce a real impact was a primary quality among the best performers."*

Learning to prioritize is one of the critical skills that you should commit yourself to mastering as you reenter the business world. You will have to learn the tough lesson that key long-term priorities cannot be sacrificed for short-term results or the quick satisfaction of completing less critical jobs.

The point I want to make here is that prioritization is more than just a good personal habit — it is a vital professional skill which plays a critical role in planning and implementing business strategy — and to be a winning manager, you've got to get very good at it.

Strategic Thinking

Now let's talk about strategic thinking. That's a subject for a whole week of meetings. So I had better prioritize and focus on developing the skill.

I can't tell you how many performance reviews I have read over the years in which a competent manager was described as a strong operating manager, but an average strategic thinker. What a shame. What a waste. Don't let that happen to you.

Good strategic thinking comes more easily to some people than to others, but it is an acquired skill, and it can be learned, but it takes enormous personal discipline.

One of the reasons is that our instincts, and sometimes our convictions, are not always strategic.

It is easy for people who have not mastered the skill of strategic thinking to confuse strategy with objectives, or with the execution of objectives, and in the process, wind up managing their business or function without a clear strategy or with the wrong strategy.

It is even easier for certain kinds of managers to formulate a losing strategy with great zeal. These are managers who have a superficial knowledge of the facts of their business, have a misguided view of the strength of their competition or a limited understanding of the options available to them.

Let's define a couple of things here

Strategic planning is a complex process designed to determine the direction a company or business will take, where it wants to end up and how it intends to get there. By its very definition, strategic planning is a selective process. You make choices from options developed within a variety of feasible scenarios.

Strategic thinking is the mental process that produces strategic direction and strategic plans. All of the well-known authors that I've read on this subject agree that, while some people are better at it than others, strategic thinking is an acquired skill. Like so many things, you only become professional at strategic thinking by mastering the fundamentals.

My advice is to try and train yourself to think strategically about every important decision in your life. There is no better way to practice the art of strategic thinking than on yourself. And it is fun sometimes. Try to think strategically about your career plan, about your free time, about your finances, your civic or volunteer activities, even your social life. In other words, the things you think about a lot.

However, the best way that I know of developing strategic thinking skills is to get into the right kind of work in whatever business you enter. People ask me where is the best place to start a career in a company, and I usually say any place that exposes you to combat. It doesn't matter what discipline you're in, or what business you're in, you need to learn how to win against someone or some force that is trying to beat you. You need to get into a situation where results of your efforts can be measured and where the soundness of your own strategic thinking can be tested in a real competitive environment.

People sometimes refer to the early training at Procter & Gamble as boot camp. Well, it isn't dancing school, but it does serve the purpose of preparing our young people for combat. I think it helps produce winning managers, who learn how to think and plan strategically at a high level of professional skill.

Personal Growth

Here's another point I want to make about skill development, and your choice of where to work in whatever business you enter. Work for people who care about your progress — not just your performance, but your progress, your growth. There is a big difference.

At Procter & Gamble, progress of the individual is part of the management culture. Nobody gets anywhere in our Company who doesn't care about progress of his subordinates. We are a promotion--f-om within Company, so the growth and advancement of people at all levels is critical to our survival. We can't afford to have anyone in the chain who isn't good at that, or doesn't work at it, or who doesn't get results.

Many organizations don't have that commitment, and you could find yourself in a real crack if you are not careful. There are bosses out there who don't really care whether their people get promoted or not. I've even seen it occasionally in our Company.

It is human nature that people want to keep the good producers for themselves, within their groups. But when it leads to holding good people back, that's when you lose good people.

The woods are also full of managers who don't know how to develop people. They can run things. They can get performance out of their organizations. They can motivate people to work hard. But, they don't know how to make people grow. They don't have mentor skills and instincts. Your growth is a very personal process, so choose wisely, and during your job interviews, ask prospective bosses to tell you about their track record at developing winning managers for their company.

Character

Now, I want to wind up with a few comments on personal character traits that you can work to develop as you grow and learn to win as a manager.

I'm not going to sermonize on the importance of honesty, ethics and respect and obedience for the law. If you don't have those qualities at this point, then I can't help you. But, even people of essentially sound character can fail for one reason or another — can fail to develop the traits that make them winners in management. I'd like to talk about just two elements of personal character that can make you a better manager, make you a winning manager. One is social intelligence. The other is trust.

Social Intelligence

Readers Digest recently published an article called *Why Smart People Fail*, which was the condensed version of a book by Carole Hyatt and Linda Gottlieb. In it, they discuss a very important character trait that is often overlooked in the development of young managers. They call it social intelligence — and define it this way:

> *"You can have great academic intelligence and still lack social intelligence — the ability to be a good listener, to be sensitive toward others, to give and take criticism well. People with high social intelligence admit their mistakes, take their share of blame, and move on. They know how to build team support."*

As in the case of strategic thinking and prioritization, social intelligence in the judgment of Hyatt and Gottlieb is an acquired skill. They say, *"The more you practice, the better you get. Like good manners, it can be learned."* I agree with that. I really do. I also believe that one of the most important benefits of developing social intelligence is that it helps make the people working for you want you to succeed. If your people want you to succeed and if they want to work for you, they will try harder to win. If people don't like you, or don't respect your character, they may help you fail, no matter how brilliant you are.

My point here is that good character traits need to be developed, and all of us very early on need to identify and correct any flaws that might stand in the way of our growth as managers.

"You can have great academic intelligence and still lack social intelligence — the ability to be a good listener, to be sensitive toward others, to give and take criticism well. People with high social intelligence admit their mistakes, take their share of blame, and move on. They know how to build team support."

Trust

Trust is a character trait that does not come easily to many people, believe it or not. But I believe that winning managers inherently trust the judgment, competence and integrity of their subordinates and are successful because they communicate that feeling to their people as part of the winning spirit they create.

Losing managers, on the other hand, are often inherently distrustful of the judgment, competence or integrity of their people, and they inevitably transmit that feeling much to their own detriment, and to the detriment of the enterprise.

Understand that I am not talking about blind, unquestioned, hands-off, let-your-people-run-wild trust. I am talking about developing the capacity to convey to people the trust that they have earned through their efforts and their performance. Think about trust. It's important, and it can help you become a winner.

Learn to Win

I hope I've given you some thoughts to ponder here today. Here's the net of what I've been saying:

Success in management is a win/lose process, and you have to learn how to become a winning manager. It's not something that most people just get out of bed and do. It all begins with attitude, striving to attain professionalism and embracing winning as a way of life.

It is sort of an inner game, an inner way of being that comes out naturally in your work ethic and your approach to your job. You can develop winning qualities and skills in your personal life and reapply them in your work.

Winning requires intense effort to develop acquired skills, particularly strategic skills which are not always well taught. Therefore, the kind of job you choose, and the kind of people you work for, can have an important bearing on your early development and progress. Finally, don't ignore the development of your personal character no matter how well you rate yourself, or how successful you've been in life thus far. The world of business will bring new stresses and new interpersonal relationships into your life, and unless you happen to be perfect, you're going to have to work on yourself as you grow.

Most importantly, though, have fun. Have confidence in your judgment when you know you're right, and win.

Thank you.

E. L. Artzt

Cornerstone Principles: Quality, Competitive Advantage, Integrity

November 7, 1991

This talk was delivered at Procter & Gamble's Annual Year-End Meeting of Employees in Cincinnati.

Procter & Gamble Principles

I think it's always fitting to close these meetings with thoughts about the key Procter & Gamble principles that underlie everything we do. I am very much aware that a lot of change is going on in our Company — and change — particularly in combination with some of the external events of the past year — causes some people to ask, "Is our Company changing?"

My answer is, "Yes, we are changing the way we work, but our principles and values are timeless, and they must never change."

I see three underlying principles as the guideposts of our Company's business philosophy. There are others, but three stand out in my mind as critical to our success.

The first is quality.
This is our positioning principle.

The second is competitive advantage.
This is our focusing principle.

The third is integrity.
This is our foundation principle — the one that defines our ethics and our character and the kind of company we want to be.

Quality is the essence of Procter & Gamble's positioning as a business enterprise. We started out selling soap and candles of high quality at good value, and that positioning principle has carried through to this day — in the kinds of brands we sell, in the kinds of people we hire, in the kinds of plants we operate. That's why Total Quality, which extends into all of our work systems, is such a good fit for our Company.

Competitive advantage is our focusing principle. Virtually everything we do should be driven by the objective of gaining competitive advantage. Every job in this Company can be done better than it is being done by our best competitor somewhere else.

It is the cumulative effect of hundreds of small competitive advantages that will enable us to achieve our financial goals, regardless of the economic environment in which we find ourselves.

If we do this, we will automatically develop the outward focus we need to succeed in an ever-shrinking, faster-moving global market. Many parts of our Company today are following this principle extremely well.

My goal is to get our whole Company focused on gaining competitive advantage, so that all of our energy is unleashed against our consumers and our customers, at the expense of our competitors.

Our third principle, integrity, is the foundation principle that embodies the values that have guided Procter & Gamble people for 154 years. Honesty, fair dealing, concern and respect for our people and a determination to always try to do the right thing.

These are the kinds of foundation principles that have been handed down through the generations, and they must and will be preserved as an integral part of our Company's character as long as we are in business.

Our long-held belief of always trying to do the right thing is worth an added comment. That means a lot more than just doing what it takes to stay out of trouble.

It means doing what common sense says is ethically correct for a company of high character. RR Deupree, one of our distinguished former Chairmen, said, "We try to do the right thing. Of course, we'll make mistakes. We may get off the beam, but we'll get right back on again."

That's our Company philosophy, that's my philosophy and that's the way all of us should think and conduct ourselves as Procter & Gamble people.

The Role of the Individual

During the past several months, I've had the pleasure of holding group luncheon meetings with a number of our employees. I intend to continue that practice, and I hope that over the course of the year, I'll have an opportunity to talk to many more of you in an informal setting, where I can listen to your questions and ideas and we can communicate our thinking on key issues face-to-face.

One subject that we have talked frequently at these luncheon groups is the role of the individual in the success of our Company. This is a subject that nearly every Procter & Gamble Chief Executive has commented on at some time or another in these annual meetings.

I suspect that this is because our Company is, first and foremost, a Company of individuals who succeed through individual ideas, individual initiative, individual leadership and, perhaps most important of all, individual accountability.

It seems that throughout our history, when the Company has gone through a series of structural organizational changes, the role of the individual has lost some of its focus and has needed to be reasserted to ensure that our change is balanced.

"Teamwork is fundamental to our high commitment work systems. It is fundamental to project management and to global planning."

If you think back, we have evolved from a Company of highly insular departments, to a Company of divisions, to a Company of smaller business units, organized along business category lines in both the United States and overseas. The resulting deinsularism has been healthy.

The creation of multi-functional matrices and teams has also been a healthy part of the deinsularization of the Company. Teamwork is fundamental to our high-commitment work systems. It is fundamental to project management and to global planning.

At the same time, it is good to remember that it is individual creativity, and individual leadership, and ultimately, individual accountability, that have always given this Company its great strength. If you read the speeches and writings of our Chief Executives over the years, as I have, you will find a very consistent thread on this score.

Nearly 40 years ago, Neil McElroy, then CEO of the Company, said, "Organization structure at P&G primarily exists as a framework for the development of individuals." Howard Morgens echoed this belief in many of his talks, and in 1987, John Smale said, "All of the examples of which we are proud, that have characterized the innovative nature of the Company, are products of individuals."

"Sometimes they are sparked by the involvement of others and by teams of people around, but they flow from individuals. As much as any Company of this size can be, this Company is the epitome of individuality."

My sense is that it is time to again remind ourselves of the need to reassert the integrity of the role of the individual in the management process of our Company.

At Procter & Gamble, individual creativity, expression and personal leadership are highly valued traits, and we encourage you to display them. Our expectation also is that each individual feel accountable and be accountable for results in their part of the business, whether the circumstances involve a business team, a project team or their individual daily work.

Following one of our recent group lunches in which we talked about this subject, Randy Potts, Director-Product Supply in the Food Sector, wrote me a note, and he has given me his permission to read you this excerpt, and I quote:

> "Your comment regarding the role of the individual was very clear and one I support. Establishing individual accountability is essential to achieve results. This in no way detracts from the synergistic contributions teams make to these results, but does establish clear singular leadership responsibility for the results."

So there you go, Randy, you've gone down in history, along with McElroy, Morgens and Smale, as one of the articulators of the role of the individual at Procter & Gamble.

Our Company has sound strategies. We have great people. We have a deep tradition of integrity and of doing the right thing for the long term. We respect the individual, and we have a culture of change that will enable us to excel in this current environment of uncertainty — but it will take the very best from each of us, working together to achieve our goals.

Knowing the kind of people you are, I'm counting on you, with a feeling of great confidence, that you will do your part — and I will do my part. I promise you that.

A Matter of Conscience

October 8, 1992

Mr. Artzt delivered this speech in New York City
upon accepting the Annual Award from the
Appeal of Conscience Foundation.

Thank you, Rabbi Schneier. I'm honored to receive this award, and I accept it with special thanks to my family and to my many colleagues at Procter & Gamble, who deserve a large measure of any recognition that I may receive.

I happen to be fortunate enough to have spent nearly 40 years working for a Company whose central and overriding principle is to always try to do the right thing.

We may not always succeed — but that deeply instilled sense of corporate conscience has provided a framework in our Company in which individuals of all backgrounds, all nationalities and all persuasions are bound together. As a product of that environment, I am proud to represent our more than 100,000 P&G employees here tonight.

I want to congratulate the men and women of the Appeal of Conscience Foundation, and particularly Rabbi Schneier, on your outstanding purpose and impressive record of achievement. Each of us is born, I believe, with a need to help make the world a better place than the one we found — better in terms of the physical environment, better in the way we deal with one another as individuals, better in the way nations act toward other nations and toward their own people. Institutions like the Appeal of Conscience Foundation help meet this need, and I'm proud to be a part of that process here tonight.

Thinking About Conscience

One cannot receive an award from an organization with "conscience" in its name without thinking deeply about the meaning of conscience, and its role in our lives and its role in our society.

As a businessman, I often deal with social issues from the standpoint of moral and ethical responsibility, economic necessity and, of course, legal obligation. But conscience is a deeper human trait, and perhaps the most difficult of all to instill in an entire society.

Why is that? Well — conscience is not something we are all automatically born with. We're born with the capacity to develop conscience — but we need help. Help through example from our parents — learning from our teachers — guidance from our religious institutions — and effective leadership from our governments. And, we must have that help in the very earliest stage of learning... when we are children.

Children are the key to using the power of conscience to change the world. As we think about the moral education of the world's children, what are the priorities?

Human rights and religious freedom — two focal points of this Foundation's mission — rank at the highest level of moral priority. But there is yet another area of need — another, where the power of conscience can make a difference. It is the environment in which we all live.

The Environment —
A Matter of Conscience

The creation of a global conscience toward environmental responsibility is one of the most urgent priorities of our time. We are using up our planet. We are abusing nature — both out of ignorance and out of disregard for its fragility — to the point where the quality of life awaiting future unborn generations could be seriously threatened.

That worries me, as I know it worries most of you. And like you, I have a strong sense of commitment to protecting our environment, which I pursue privately and through our Company. The environment is a matter of conscience with me, but I was not always that way.

When I was a young boy growing up in Los Angeles in the '30s, virtually every home had a backyard incinerator. I remember that one of my daily chores was to burn the trash. Can you picture 500,000 backyard incinerators burning trash in Los Angeles? We all thought we were doing the right thing. We were helping the community reduce garbage collection costs.

But I was damaging the environment, and I didn't know it. I was conscience-free because, environmentally, I was ignorant. Millions of people are still like that today.

Yet, whole nations have developed a strong environmental conscience, but not without education and not without pain. Germany is a case in point. Germany today is one of the world's most environmentally conscious nations, driven by stringent laws and regulations. A very strong informed national conscience has developed, but it was not always that way.

A few weeks ago, I had the privilege of meeting with Chancellor

Kohl in Bonn, and here's an interesting personal anecdote he shared with our group.

He said,

"In 1949, when I was 19 years old, I made my first political speech. If I had talked about the environment, a promising political career would have ended right then. People were more anxious to see that smoke stacks produced smoke, because it would say that we are working again."

The Chancellor added that, "Had we known then what we know now, we could have saved enormous sums of money preventing the problems that we now have to fix."

And now, there is hope that in the future all nations will know what they should have known. This past June, 182 nations and 105 heads of state convened the Earth Summit in Rio, and formed the beginnings of a global partnership committed to sustainable development. What a great step forward.

But it's not enough. If we really are going to make a lasting change — then all the world's children must be taught to love nature and to respect the fragility of our environment — not just as a matter of survival — but as a matter of conscience.

The Role of Business

Here is where business and industry can make a real contribution.
For example, at P&G, we sponsor a primary school program
called Planet Patrol. This teaching unit provides schools with
information and materials to explain environmental issues like
solid waste, recycling and composting.

Planet Patrol provides teachers with hands-on environmental
projects ranging from simple worksheets to keep a daily log of how
much each family throws away — to the construction of a classroom
compost pile — all teaching tools to help educators teach their
students about the importance of environmental responsibility.

More than 6 million students throughout the United States have
been involved in the Planet Patrol program. We're also expanding
it to Canada and looking at other countries around the world.
Other companies have similar classroom programs, but we need
much more of a corporate effort, and we need it everywhere.

Finally, we adults need to become living examples of the
environmental conscience we want our children to embrace. This
is no small task, because it requires a voluntary re-education of
ourselves. It means we have to change our own behavior patterns
and adapt our own values to reflect the belief that respect for
nature is as sacred a trust as respect for family, God and country.

A Moral Obligation

It is our moral obligation as adults to do all we can to protect our
children's future — and so we must endow the children of our
planet with a deep and unshakeable environmental conscience.
Conscience is a wonderful thing. It can change the world. It

can do what no laws — no rules — no threat of punishment or penalty can ever do — because it is an enduring, self-regulating, positive force.

We must bring the power of that force of conscience to future generations through the education of our children — so that this beautiful, naturally abundant world of ours may be protected for all time.

I accept this award with my personal, continued commitment to advance this goal. And, I thank you again for this honor.

E. L. Artzt

Section

05

A Company of Individuals

November 5, 1992

This is an edited version of a talk delivered at Procter & Gamble's Annual Year-End Meeting of Employees in Cincinnati.

It is individual initiative that has always been at the root of P&G's success. Different people have said it in different ways over the years.

In 1962, P&G Chairman Neil McElroy said very simply, "Our Company is a company of individuals. "A decade later, Brad Butler, another former P&G chairman, said, "The driving force which makes for success is the force of an individual mind and of individual energy, directed perhaps by an organization, amplified perhaps by an organization, but coming from an individual."

And in 1987, John Smale touched on the same theme. He said, "I think the Company from the very beginning has by its nature tried to encourage the expression of individuality. How else do you account for a guy like RR Deupree who goes to work for the Company at 12 years of age and then heads up the business?"

Over the years, I've come to understand the fundamental truth of these statements. This is not a company of ordinary individuals. It's an organization of high-energy, creative, articulate people who like to set higher standards for themselves than anyone else can set for them.

This is the reason we've been so successful. Isn't it amazing, when you think about all the different people who have worked for Procter & Gamble over the last century and a half — more than half a million — so many individuals, so unique and so endowed with capacity. All so different — yet they have perpetuated a common standard of excellence across businesses of all kinds, across continents, across cultures, across decades, even centuries.

And with all these differences, we've consistently doubled our business about every 10 years.

It's worked because P&G people throughout the years and around the world have been bound together by the timeless principles of integrity, respect for the individual and doing the right thing.

It starts with the people we hire. People of character, intelligence and energy. People with a history of performing to high personal standards. We're a Company of achievers.

And all of the P&G leaders back through our history knew one thing for sure. If you put together an organization of achievers, you must create an environment in which they can achieve — an atmosphere that fosters expression and creativity. An atmosphere in which criticisms get heard, ideas get tried and proposals get forwarded. An atmosphere in which individual initiative is encouraged and produces action, and where individual achievement gets recognized.

How do you create such an atmosphere? Well, organization is a big part of it. We must have organizations that give us structure and discipline without bureaucracy and gridlock. We must have matrices to give us breadth in our planning, and to drive out insular complexity. And we must have teams to give us coordination and efficiency and to stimulate input from every function. But all of these constructs are merely the framework to enhance and empower the contributions of the individual.

To create such an atmosphere, we must do all we can — through training, career development, mentoring, all the things I talked about just a moment ago — to help every P&G employee succeed.

Recognizing Individual Achievement

Then, we must recognize achievement, and we're starting to do that in some interesting ways. Not just in recognizing the big wins, which are great to celebrate, but also, the sustained achievement of individuals over time at all levels.

There are a lot of ways to recognize contribution. We need to do it day-to-day — with regular feedback ... informal celebration ... a special note of thanks.

We can also do it by changing organization structure to reward sustained individual achievement. For example, just yesterday, Gordon Brunner announced the creation of a new technical career progression system within R&D. It's a contribution-based system for all R&D people. For the first time, it creates a technical career progression track where people can advance based on their technology contributions, not just their administrative or managerial ability.

We think this not only provides important opportunities for added recognition, it also provides added motivation to increase the innovative output of our research organization.

We also need to do more to recognize individual contribution through formal recognition programs. R&D has led the way here, as well, with the creation of the Victor Mills Society. The Society began two years ago in honor of the extraordinary contributions Vic made during his 35-year career at P&G.

For those of you who don't know Vic, he was probably the Company's most prolific inventor. Our detergent spray drying process, Pampers, Duncan Hines cake mixes, Jif and Pringles — all come from innovations led by Vic Mills. All in all, Vic has 25 patents in his name and still leads an active life at the age of 95.

The second Vic Mills Society ceremony was held just yesterday. We inducted six new members, bringing the total to 18, again reinforcing the importance to our business of empowering individual initiative at all levels of the Company.

Last year marked the inauguration of Product Supply's Worldwide Technology Achievement Awards, which recognize both individual and team achievements in Product Supply — achievements based on outstanding technical mastery in Product Supply.

Our newest recognition program is called The Chairman's Club. It recognizes members of our Sales organization whose leadership and initiative have resulted in breakthrough results for the Company. The first U.S. Chairman's Club dinner — The Night of Champions — was held here in Cincinnati in September. And this program will be worldwide next year.

I've been able to participate in all three of these recognition events, and I can tell you that they have been moving experiences — because, they really capture the spirit of Procter & Gamble. As I said in my remarks at last year's Product Supply awards program, "The essential strength of our Company comes from the mind, the brilliance, the restless dissatisfaction and the leadership of individuals."

Individuals like new Vic Mills Society member, Toan Trinh, a chemist born and raised in Hanoi, Vietnam. Toan was one of the last to get out prior to the fall of Saigon during the Vietnam War, and in 1976, he joined P&G. Over the years, Toan has received 25 patents in seven areas of research. His technologies are the basis for the superior softening performance of our world liquid fabric softeners. And the basis for our world leadership share of 33%.

It's individuals like Jean Webers, also a new Vic Mills honoree, who joined the Company as a Technician at our European

Technical Center in 1972. He has 23 patents to his name, and his innovative capability stems from a flair for making unusual connections across very different fields, from chemistry to chocolate processing. Jean is the father of the builder technology in our world liquid detergents, and he also helped develop the world process for compact detergents.

Another wonderful example is Norbert DeWitte, a Product Supply Technology Achievement Award winner. Norbert joined P&G in 1962 in Benelux Purchasing. Over a 10-year period, he changed the rules of the game in European laundry chemical supply. He moved boldly to break the stranglehold held by the European chemical cartel, creating a truly competitive supply environment in Europe — and saving the Company more than $1 billion so far.

And then in U.S. Sales, there's Cheryl Scales, a new Chairman's Club member. Cheryl joined P&G in 1984 and is now District Manager in Food and Beverage National Accounts in Dallas. When Cheryl picked up responsibility for the largest convenience store wholesaler in the U.S. last year, she had a tough challenge because our business had been declining an average of 5% a year for each of the last five years.

Cheryl used her outstanding selling skills to turn this business around so that it's on track to double by the end of next year — and she has agreement from the top management of this account to a plan to deliver an additional 2 million cases.

Finally, here's a good example of how the initiative of an individual can lead a strong team to extraordinary achievement. Bill Jacoby, a national account manager for the Commercial Services Product Group, led the biggest single sale in the history of his division. Bill and his team showed McDonald's how they could improve the quality of their fried foods and, at the same time, lower costs. As a result, P&G became the first new supplier of frying oils to the McDonald's Corporation in its 37-year history. This sale will produce 1 million incremental cases for the Company in the next 12 months.

This is the kind of performance that people all over our Company are turning in day after day. But all too often, we fail to stop long enough to recognize their performance. And that recognition is important.

A Sense of Belonging

Listen, for example, to what Lou Bruno, our U.S. Paper Sales Unit Manager from Bradenton, Florida, had to say about his Chairman's Club Award. He sent me this letter a few days after the ceremony, and Lou has given me permission to share it with you:

I don't think I can express what a rewarding experience it was to attend the "Night of Champions" dinner. I have a tremendous amount of respect and admiration for the National Sales Managers and Division Managers that I have worked with during my 15+ years with the Company.

The opportunity to accept the Chairman's Club Award with these managers in attendance gave me the greatest sense of accomplishment, recognition and acceptance that I have ever experienced. For the first time in 15 years as a manager in P&G sales, I felt a sense of belonging to the Company, the depths of which I have never felt before. I felt that my contributions were being recognized and appreciated, that the Company was somehow smaller and more close-knit than I had previously imagined and that I was going to be able to stay with the Company for the duration of my business life. I left with a sense of renewed commitment and enthusiasm, ready to take on the next 15+ years as a manager in P&G sales.

As Lou makes so clear, recognition counts. It's important. It makes a difference. So, I want to challenge all of our organizations to establish a formal recognition process. One that rewards the sustained achievements of individuals. Let's do it right across the Company.

A Challenge to P&G People

As I said at the beginning, individual initiative and creativity have always been at the root of P&G's success. In fact, they are the sparks that have always fueled our Company's remarkable ability to reinvent itself.

Something I heard Neil McElroy say once captures it best: "The people of a business," he said, "are motivated to their highest possible level of performance only if they have maximum freedom and incentive, only if they are given plenty of individual responsibility, and only if superior performance is suitably recognized."

Neil McElroy said that almost 30 years ago — and it's just as true today as it was then.

But there are some parts of the world where it's an entirely new idea. For years under communism, people in state-owned businesses in Czechoslovakia, Hungary and Poland weren't encouraged to innovate. They weren't encouraged to take initiative. They weren't encouraged to challenge the status quo.
So, for many of our employees in our new businesses in Eastern Europe, P&G's focus on individual initiative and contribution is truly something new. And welcome.

Michael Andronikov is a great example. Michael was one of the very first employees we hired in Czechoslovakia, shortly after we opened our office there last fall. He's part of our Finance organization and, with a year under his belt now, is considered a veteran of our Czechoslovakian business. But his perspective on Procter & Gamble is still fresh. Let me share with you something he said recently:

> "Before coming to P&G, I worked at a state bank. At a state enterprise, with its big bureaucracy, you have no responsibility and see no results of your own work. No one wants you to express your opinions.
>
> When privatization came to Czechoslovakia, I wanted to work for the best company and to see the results of my work. Here at P&G, I can recommend a plan and see the results of what I've recommended. I can bring my own ideas and approaches. I can influence the business. This is new to us.

It's in that spirit that I'd like to leave you with a challenge — to do what these Vic Mills recipients and the Product Supply honorees and the Chairman's Club winners have done: reaffirm your commitment to individual initiative. Find what needs to be changed...refocused...reshaped...in your job and in your organization ... and then change it.

Ed Artzt

06

Stop the Hate

January 16, 1993

Mr. Artzt delivered this speech in Atlanta, Georgia, at the Martin Luther King Jr. Salute to Greatness dinner, which he chaired.

I want to say how honored I am to be here tonight.

This is a very special occasion, because we're commemorating so many important milestones — the celebration of Dr. King's birth 64 years ago, the 10th anniversary of the King holiday, the 25th anniversary of the King Center, and the 30th anniversary of the March on Washington.

It's altogether fitting, on such an occasion, that we come together to salute not only Dr. King's greatness but also the greatness of the men and women who marched beside him, who worked with him and who have continued the dream.

It's also important, I believe, that as we reflect on all these milestones, we again ask ourselves the question that Dr. King posed a quarter century ago: Where do we go from here?

But before we can begin to answer that question, we need to look first at where we are.

I'm not an expert — I have no claim to wisdom or truth on the issue of race relations, but as I look around at the racial climate that exists in our country today, it's clear to me that we haven't made the kind of progress Dr. King hoped for.

There are successes to point to, of course, and we should celebrate them. Real progress has been made in the legal protection of civil rights. And we're seeing greater levels of meaningful diversity in many segments of our society. As a result, African Americans are making important strides in business — including the corporate world — in government, in education, in all sectors of society. But I still don't feel very good at all about where we are.

I come from Cincinnati — a good town, with good people — a good place for everyone to work and live — but we've just had our noses rubbed in the brutal reality of racism in the 1990s. I'm humiliated. I'm angry. I'm fed up with it — and more important, I want to do something about it.

Racism is still very much a reality. It's everywhere — it's in the home, it's in the streets and it's in the workplace. It really hasn't ever gone away. And we — and I mean all of us — must acknowledge that reality before we can change it. But all too often, well-intentioned people simply refuse to face the truth. They permit themselves to be comforted by the belief that anti-discrimination laws and company diversity policies in the business world have put an end to overt racial prejudice in our country.

This is nothing new. Dr. King made the same observation 25 years ago. He said, "Laws are passed in a crisis mood after a Birmingham or a Selma, but no substantial fervor survives the formal signing of legislation. The recording of the law in itself is treated as the reality of the reform."

That was true in 1967. And, sadly, it's still true today. We, as a general public, believe in the principles of racial equality. We're outraged when we see examples of hate crimes and racist brutality. And I can tell you that everyone in our town cringed with humiliation at the events there recently. The baseball issue was bad enough, but the sight of a Ku Klux Klan cross in our city square at Christmastime surely must have shocked the conscience of every decent citizen.

Maybe — just maybe — this is what we needed to get our act together, and strike out at some of the root causes of racism, as well as its effects. But, as Dr. King reminded us, once this land of atrocious behavior has been curbed, we tend to settle easily into complacency.

And this complacency feeds racism just as much as an offensive remark. It may not gain the notoriety of blatant racism, but it is equally and perhaps even more destructive — because it exists just under the surface, submerged by denial and protected by the indifference of a society that responds only to the most sensational racial offenses.

This is where we need to make our greatest progress — to change not just how we act, but more importantly, how we think and how we feel about race. You can mandate behavior, but you have to change attitudes. And that takes a lot more doing than getting a law passed, and a lot deeper change than simply establishing diversity in the workplace.

I've come to realize that the most subtle forms of racism are sometimes the most destructive, especially in the workplace. Young Black managers I've talked with refer to it as the "pain threshold" — the added burden that results from having one's opinions discounted, from failing to receive deserved credit or recognition, or having to work to a different standard than one's peers and seldom receiving the benefit of the doubt in close-call situations. Subtle, debilitating, largely unrecognized racism. We have to deal with this.

What do we need to do?

First, we must take every opportunity to confront racism when we see it. We must look for these subtle, debilitating practices, and make it clear that they are not acceptable in our organizations and in our homes. We must make every effort to educate one another about racism and its consequences ... then do all we can to overcome the denial that perpetuates racist behavior.

But frankly, if we're going to make truly lasting change, then we have to stop racism before it starts — by doing a far better job of teaching our children to respect and to value racial, religious and cultural differences between people in our diverse society.

One of the most compelling observations Dr. King made is that "racial understanding is not something we find but something we must create."

We begin life with neither racial prejudice nor racial understanding. But the absence of these feelings creates a void — a void that can be filled with disrespect or even hate — a void that gets filled on street corners and playgrounds and around family dinner tables where children hear the things that create lasting imprints on their minds.

But I believe the void can be filled another way — with understanding — the kind of understanding that breeds respect forracial and cultural differences and forms the human values that will guide children throughout their lives.

One thing is certain: That void will be filled one way or the other. If we hesitate, yet another generation will be lost. We can't wait. Life's too short.

That very message was driven home to me just a couple of weeks ago when I saw this public service announcement, sponsored by the Leadership Conference Education Fund.

[LCEF Public Service Announcement, "Life's Too Short. Stop the Hate." is shown.]

That spot got my attention. It affected me, and I knew that the idea behind it could have a lasting effect on children. So we got in touch with the Leadership Conference to learn more about this campaign.

I'm sure many of you are familiar with it — some of you may have been involved in developing it — in fact, Ralph Neas, the Fund's Executive Director and Karen McGill Arrington, the deputy director, are here with us tonight.

But let me briefly describe what they're doing. This public service campaign, which consists of the TV spot as well as print and radio ads, was a response to last summer's riots. It's part of a long-term informational campaign designed to increase awareness of racism and to educate people about the value of racial diversity.

This is an important program, but what I find even more encouraging is that the Leadership Conference is also planning another phase of this campaign, targeted to children.

Their plan is to launch a Children's Campaign to help kids create the kind of racial understanding Dr. King talked about. They want to develop a series of videotaped lessons for classrooms and are talking with Fred Rogers, of *Mr. Rogers' Neighborhood*, about how to get that started. They're also planning to develop supplemental materials to help parents reinforce the lessons their children learn at school — things like storybooks and comic books, as well as a handbook for parents on *How to Talk to Your Child About Racism*.

When I learned about the Children's Campaign, I saw it as an opportunity to salute the greatness of Martin Luther King Jr. by answering his question — Where Do We Go From Here? — with a promise to our children.

That promise is that we will not hesitate to fill the void in our children's hearts — with love instead of hate, understanding instead of ignorance.

In that spirit, the Procter & Gamble Fund has agreed to underwrite a major portion of the Children's Campaign with a $500,000 grant — and Mrs. King and Jesse Hill have agreed to join me as principal advisors in the development of this program.

I know this is just a small step. But I'm convinced it's an important one — and I urge all of you to get involved in this program and others like it.

If we can change the hearts of today's children, we'll influence the minds of tomorrow's adults. Thank you.

Unchanging Values in Changing Times

November 4, 1993

This talk was delivered at Procter & Gamble's Annual Year-end Meeting of Employees in Cincinnati.

I want to conclude with some comments about the Company's values.

We have said over and over this week that we must change the way we work in order to bring better value to our consumers. We're changing systems, structures, procedures and processes. We're doing all of this to ensure that we stay competitive in a highly value-conscious world. We're doing all of this to ensure that we continue to win in the marketplace over the long term.

At the same time, we're dedicated to those simple values that have made this Company truly unique since its founding in 1837. Our values go back to the principles of just and right dealing upon which William Procter and James Gamble built this Company. These are the core beliefs, the ideas and principles that guide our actions and bind us together.

I wanted to find a very personal way to express these thoughts today, and I found the inspiration I was looking for in a speech that William Cooper Procter gave to Company employees at the Music Hall here in Cincinnati in 1925. He said:

> "These meetings are for one purpose — an inspirational one. I would not, if I could, attempt to make an inspirational speech, because I do not think it is necessary. If I can get you to see the Procter & Gamble Company and its relation to industry and to society, as I see it, you will need no other inspiration."

1993 is a special year for me. Next month will mark my 40th year with the Company, and like many of you, I can remember my first day like it was yesterday. That day, I attended the North Los Angeles Year-End District Sales Meeting. I was a new salesman, and I had not yet sold one case of soap—I was pretty nervous and, as you can imagine, very attentive. I remember thinking, "These people like each other. They care about one another, and they love the Company."

I felt that way 40 years ago, and I feel that way today.

As the years have gone by, and I have had the experience of working in almost every division of the Company throughout our worldwide operations, my enthusiasm and affection for this Company has deepened into a feeling of great pride.

I am proud to work for a company that wants to be the best, wants to be the leader in everything it does and embraces the high standards necessary to consistently achieve high goals. We all work for a winner.

I work for a company that places integrity above all else — a company that believes in always trying to do the right thing. Always obeys the law — even when competitors might not, always practices fair dealing with partners, customers, suppliers and agents.

I work for a company that operates by principle and is willing to forego expedient compromise to preserve its principles—a company that stands up for its principles, even under criticism, political pressure or coercion—a company that would rather lose a large order or even a large customer than make a payment under the table or discriminate between customers. I have always admired our Company's incessant courage and conviction under difficult odds.

I work for a company that places the quality and safety of its products above all other considerations—a company that would voluntarily withdraw a multi-million-dollar brand from the market rather than risk the health of a single consumer.

"I work for a company that places character above all other qualities in the people it hires — a company that honors and respects individual initiative at every level of the business."

I work for a company that is unequivocally proactive and not just responsive in its efforts to clear up and preserve the world's environment.

I work for a company that places character above all other qualities in the people it hires — a company that honors and respects individual initiative at every level of the business.

I'm proud to work for a company so dedicated to the development of its people that it has successfully built its organization, promoting from within for over 150 years — a company that has always believed in the fair treatment of its employees.

Sixty-eight years ago, in a similar meeting like this, these values were reaffirmed by William Cooper Procter. All of those P&G people are gone from the Company. Sixty-eight years from now, in a meeting like this, I think P&G people will gather here to discuss these same values, but all of us will be gone from the Company.

The Company's people come and go, but the values that bind us together are permanent. They will never change.

These are more than ethical principles. They are good business. They are rules of living that make one's career rewarding beyond all material gain.

This is one of the truly great business institutions in the world.

I've heard it said that because of our strict ethical principles, the Company has sometimes had to win its success with one hand tied behind its back. In the long run, if you learn how to win that way, you are awfully hard to beat.

Section

08

Opportunity 2000

September 29, 1994

Mr. Artzt delivered this speech in Washington, D.C., upon accepting the Opportunity 2000 Award, the U.S. Department of Labor's highest award for equal employment opportunity. This award was presented to Procter & Gamble by Secretary of Labor Robert Reich.

Thank you, Mr. Secretary. On behalf of nearly 97,000 Procter & Gamble people around the world, I am very proud to accept this award.

This recognition means a lot to all of us because we truly believe that equal opportunity — at every level of our organization — is in our best interest as a company. It's not a matter of merely complying with government rules and regulations. It is a fundamental part of our corporate philosophy. Every P&G employee — regardless of race, gender or ethnic background — has an equal opportunity to advance and succeed.

We also see diversity in our workforce as a competitive strength. We know that when we take full advantage of the breadth of experiences, perspectives and ideas that diversity brings, we win in the marketplace.

One of the unique things about P&G is that we promote strictly from within. That makes it especially important that we provide every individual the right training, mentoring and development opportunities they need to grow — and hold their managers accountable for that. Our Company's future depends on it.

Even with a process like this, minorities and females can fall behind the benchmark of the rest of our workforce. Therefore, we monitor the advancement progress of these groups very closely to ensure the principle of equal opportunity is being served.

We think this approach makes sense for Procter & Gamble and hope that it provides a valuable model for other companies as well. American companies cannot hope to remain competitive in today's global marketplace if they limit the pool from which they find their best talent — or if they deny their best people the tools they need to develop and succeed.

We will never be satisfied with where we are. Continuous improvement is an integral part of our Company's culture. I expect our results to improve. In fact, I can guarantee it.

It's in that spirit that we accept this award, Mr. Secretary.

Thank you.

Section

09

Competitive Edge

November 3, 1994

This talk was delivered at Procter & Gamble's Annual
Year-End Meeting of Employees in Cincinnati.

We are about to close the record books on the first five years of the '90s. We're at the midpoint, so today, I want to look at our progress toward the Year 2000 goals we established five years ago. After that, I'm going to talk about what has made our Company so consistently successful.

1993/94 was an outstanding year. Earnings were up 15%, profit margins and return on equity were the highest in recent history. Cash flow from operations reached $3.6 billion — and more than $100 million in after-tax restructuring savings reached the bottom line in less than 12 months.

Getting Off To a Good Start

We're also off to a good start in the new fiscal year. Worldwide shipments for July-September were up 10%. New businesses and acquisitions accounted for 3 percentage points of that, so we're up 7% on continuing businesses — a little better than last year's overall growth rate of 5%.

The new businesses include the Schickedanz tissue business in Europe, Giorgio perfumes, our new joint ventures in China and Latin America and others.

We're starting to see good sales growth once again. July-September sales were $8.2 billion, 8% above a year ago. Last year's sales were flat, but now the divestitures of our pulp and orange juice businesses are behind us, and foreign exchange rates are reasonably stable. So sales growth is now more in line with unit volume growth.

Worldwide earnings for the July-September quarter totaled $792 million — that's up 18% — $122 million better than last year. This is a direct result of strong volume growth, the excellent job that you are doing at reducing costs, and the early savings from our restructuring.

I'll provide more detail on the July-September results in the next edition of *P&G This Quarter*. But I want to congratulate you now for your outstanding results in 1993/94 and the continuing good work you've done in the first quarter of 1994/95. It's one of our best starts in many years.

Before I go further, I'd like to comment on the Company's recent suit against Bankers Trust. We don't like to go around suing our bankers, but these people clearly qualify as an exception.

As we said in our news release, "There is a notion that end users of derivatives must be held accountable for what they buy. We agree completely, but only if the terms and risks are fully and accurately disclosed." Bankers Trust did not do that, and the result was a significant financial loss to Procter & Gamble.

We considered our decision to file suit very carefully, and I'm convinced it's the right thing to do — for the Company and for our shareholders. The suit may go on for some time, and P&G may be criticized in the press for not quietly taking our lumps and moving on. We can stand the heat. What we're doing is right.

Toward the Year 2000

Now, let's look at progress toward our Year 2000 goals. We first talked about these goals five years ago at the 1989 Year-End Meeting. We said if we continued to grow at the same compound growth rate as the 1980s, we would reach $50 billion in sales and $3 billion in earnings by the end of the decade.

On earnings, we are well ahead of that pace. In fact, we should exceed the $3 billion projection by quite a bit, so we need to reset this target to be sure it's challenging enough for the second half of the decade.

Steadily Growing Earnings

Over the last 50 years, earnings growth has averaged 10% per year. If we grow at this same rate over the remainder of the decade, earnings will exceed $4 billion — more than $1 billion above the projection that we made five years ago. This should be our minimum target. With the steps we've taken to improve the Company's cost structure and to accelerate unit volume growth, earnings should increase beyond 10% a year.

Last year, for example, earnings grew by 15%. If we can sustain this higher rate of growth during the next six years, earnings will be over $5 billion in the Year 2000.

That's $2 billion more than we were projecting at the start of the decade.

Last year, when we met here, I said P&G needs to be increasing earnings at about 15% per year to lead our industry group. We did that in 1993/94, and it has helped renew investor confidence in P&G.

Improving Shareholder Return

We used to say that doubling our volume every 10 years was the only business goal we needed to set as a Company. That made sense because we were accustomed to fairly high profit margins and very high rates of return on investments and new businesses. We had this long history that said "Grow the volume and everything else follows."

But now, the world is more complicated than that. Not all our businesses earn high margins. In fact, many new businesses lose money for an extended period of time, as we enter new geographies against entrenched competitors or new categories where we don't have a heritage of technology superiority.

So, we've had to set more focused financial goals than in the past. And today, more than ever, we have to focus on shareholder value. That's what all our effort translates into. We're tracked relentlessly by teams of market analysts who look at how the Company is managed financially. They look at the soundness of our investments, our rates of return.

These aren't the only things that count, but if P&G's financial performance does not measure up to the expectations of the people investing in our Company, then we will ultimately lose our flexibility to do the things we want to do for the long-term good of the business.

The truth is, we have not always done as well as we need to in building shareholder value. Over the past 30 years, P&G's annual total return to shareholders — that is, stock price appreciation plus dividends — has averaged only 11%. That's not bad, but it ranks us 15th among the 18-company consumer products peer group the financial community uses as a performance benchmark.

That's close to dead last among a group that includes Colgate, Gillette, Helene Curds, Kimberly-Clark, PepsiCo and Unilever — our major competitors in each sector. No P&G employee I know wants to come in 15th in an 18-horse race. I'm pleased to say, though, that we've been getting out of our rut. Over the past five years, we've ranked number three, with an average annual shareholder return of 17%.

The most important reason for this improved shareholder return relative to our peers is unproved earnings growth. Our 30-year annual earnings growth rate averaged 10%, only 12th among our peer group. Below average earnings growth — and below average total shareholder return.

Over the past five years, earnings growth has averaged 14%.
P&G ranked seventh. Better earnings growth — better shareholder return.

Over the last 12 months — that includes July-September — our
earnings growth has been 17%, and investors have responded
favorably. P&G stock has appreciated 18%, moving from about
$54 per share last year to just over $64 last Friday. Those other
consumer products companies averaged only 7% appreciation, so
we're well up there.

Increasing the Price Of P&G Stock

Now, let's take a look at what would happen to our stock price if
we reach $4 billion in earnings — our minimum target — by the
year 2000, assuming our current price-to-earnings ratio.

Our stock would be worth at least $100 per share. That's an
increase of over $35 per share over the next five years. The total
market value of Procter & Gamble would increase over $25
billion. P&G employees and retirees own 25% of our stock, so
over $6 billion of this additional value would be in the hands of
the people who either helped to build this Company in the past
or who are now creating the future. That's the way it should be.

In fact, it should be better than that. If we can continue to deliver
the 15% annual earnings growth achieved last year, our stock
would be worth at least $130 in the year 2000 — over $65 per
share higher than the current market. That adds up to over $90
billion in market value — more than double today's value. Over
$12 billion of this nearly $50 billion increase would be in the
hands of P&G employees and retirees.

Setting Higher Targets

I think we can hit this higher target. Our businesses are generally healthy and growing. Two years ago, for example, our U.S. business was soft. Shipments were flat. Last year, the business rebounded with solid growth in each quarter — particularly impressive since market sizes increased only 1% during the year. Now, the U.S. has delivered a record first quarter with shipments up 7%.

Five years ago, we said the U.S. needed to pick up its pace of growth. They're doing that.

We are also doing very well at building our businesses outside the U.S. During each of the last two years, International shipments increased 10%, with acquisitions contributing 2 percentage points of this growth. In 1994/95, International is off to an even better start, with shipments up 13% in the first quarter.

Five years ago, we said that International would be at least half of the Company's business by the end of the decade. We've already reached this objective — today, 51% of our sales come from outside the U.S. We should see International at nearly 60% of worldwide sales by the end of this decade. That's a good measure of how effectively we have been globalizing our Company.

Catching up on Sales Growth

Dollar sales is the one area where we have fallen behind the pace needed to achieve our original $50 billion projection.

A number of factors account for slower than expected sales growth. First, unfavorable currency exchange rates — in 1993/94 alone, the stronger U.S. dollar resulted in a $1.1 billion year-to-year reduction in sales. Sales also declined as we lowered our

prices to deliver better value to consumers — list prices were
down $700 million in 1993/94 alone.

In addition, inflation rates have been lower than expected. That's
good. Our original projections for the decade assumed 5%
inflation. However, inflation moderated during the last five years
and is now expected to average roughly 4% during the decade.
That one percent difference may not sound like much, but it
adds up to nearly $3 billion less in dollar sales per year by 2000.

Finally, we knew when we divested the pulp and orange juice
businesses that this would take a chunk out of our sales. But
these were not strategic businesses, and juice was quite unprofit-
able. Through divestiture, we have redeployed significant capital
in more strategic, more profitable businesses, and that will be
showing up in our results over the next five years.

We need to be cautious about too much focus on dollar sales
growth. We don't want to go out and do things to grow sales
for the wrong reasons — like increasing prices above our
costs or above the inflation rate. That wouldn't be justified. It
would create poor value, and it would hurt our business. We're
not going to do that.

At our current pace, a sales projection of $50 billion in the year
2000 would require a compound dollar sales growth rate of 9%
from now to the end of the decade. We might still get there.

But, the most important measures are whether we are sustaining
a healthy unit volume growth rate and meeting our earnings
targets. In both cases, we're doing well, so sales growth should
not be our major concern.

Delivering Restructuring Savings

We also said in 1989 that our costs were getting out of line. Our SR&A expenses were higher than some of our competitors. We could not continue to afford the organization we were building. In 1992, we determined we would have to take steps to reduce our overheads and control costs to deliver better value to the consumer and keep our brands competitively priced. This, of course, led to SGE and the plant consolidations.

These changes have been very difficult for all of us — painful but necessary. And our restructuring has been a success thus far. Savings are getting to the bottom line. And the employees who have left the Company to seek other employment have typically found new jobs quickly. The average time to re-employment is about six weeks. We repeatedly hear from other companies, consulting firms and outplacement services that P&G's treatment of employees in its restructuring was the best they have ever seen.

We've even heard this from P&G people who were affected. Peter Miller — an employee from our Quincy, MA, plant which recently closed — spoke at our Shareholders' Meeting last month. Here is what he said:

> *"The restructuring that the Company has been going through has impacted greatly on thousands of people, and it's been very, very traumatic for all of these people in different ways. I would hope that as these things happen – and we see them happening across the country in so many other companies – that companies look to Procter & Gamble as a role model in how to do this and how to handle a really difficult situation ... a very complicated, very emotional situation."*

Now, some have asked, are we there yet? Can we put this behind us and go back to business as usual? Well, we're almost there. We have achieved 89% of our SGE enrollment reduction target, and we have announced about three-quarters of the plant positions to be reduced.

I wish I could tell you that this is it — that there will never be another SGE. But I can't. I can't say "never."

I can tell you that there are no plans to do this again, and we're well positioned to avoid another major downsizing in the foreseeable future. I also know that downsizing by itself is not the answer to all our structural cost problems.

But, our competitors are getting leaner every day. So, if we're to avoid another SGE, we must continue — day in, day out — to stay sharply focused on costs, to streamline the way we work and to drive out non-value-added activities. These are the things we must do to stay ahead, to keep delivering better value, and above all, to keep building our business to provide opportunities for people to grow in the Company.

The bottom line at this midpoint of the decade is that we have a lot to feel good about. Our strategies are working. We're in a solid competitive position to keep growing. As one investment analyst said recently, "It's real easy to see that Procter & Gamble is outperforming its competitors."

Maintaining Our Momentum

The question now is, what do we need to do to maintain this growth? What will it take to sustain 15% earnings growth from year to year? How will we add 1 or even 2 billion dollars to the bottom line in the next five years? How do we keep this good thing going?

Focus. Focus on our three fundamental growth strategies:

- Building our core established businesses through product innovation.

- Expanding core businesses into new geographies.

- And entering new categories with new brands.

These strategies have been at the root of our success over the past five years and will continue to be. Yet, this Company has not just been successful for the past year or the past five years. We have a consistent record of success over more than 150 years.

Being the Best

So what is it that has made P&G so successful? What is it that binds generations of P&G people together? What is the essence of Procter & Gamble that has been handed down from one generation to the next — and has kept this Company growing over the decades?

Without question, our Company values have been of primary importance: integrity, honesty, respect for the individual and trying to do the right thing. But there is another very fundamental reason for P&G's long history of success. It is our relentless desire to be the best in everything we do — and the willingness to work together to gain the competitive edge we need to be the best.

P&G people want to be number one. And they want to stay number 1. It's an integral part of our Company culture. It is not just a slogan. At P&G, it is a way of life.

But what does it mean to be the best? How do we define it? Measure it? Sustain it?

Winning Where It Counts

We define being the best in many ways — but the payoff is just one thing — market leadership for our brands. We want to be the leader in every business in which we compete.

Not just because it feels good to be number one. It does — but we're committed to market leadership as a basic Company philosophy. It is the ultimate measure of the kind of Company we want to be.

Leadership also produces many tangible benefits.

Market leaders are generally more profitable than their competition. It's not just size or economy of scale that does it. It's a whole range of advantages that accrue to the leader. In most cases, the number one brand earns 50% to 60% of a category's total profits. The number two brand may get 20% to 30% and all the rest divide the remaining 10% to 20%.

For example — the U.S. Laundry category. Tide is the market leader. It represents about 30% of the category's total volume. But Tide earns 60% of total detergent category profits. That's how valuable market leadership is.

Fabric Conditioners — the same. Downy Liquid has a 33% market share and earns 55% of category profits.

Crest has a 36% share and earns 46% of profits.

Why is leadership so profitable? Simple. The market leader has lower costs — lower fixed costs per case, lower delivered cost per case, lower SR&A per case, lower brand support per case.

Trade customers feature market leaders more often and more prominently than number two or three brands.

In health care categories, like dentifrice or analgesics, where professional support is critical, market-leading brands are more likely to be recommended by doctors and dentists than other brands.

So, when P&G people hold themselves accountable for being the best, it's not just about pride. It's about building the business through competitive advantage. It's about beating the competition.

Measuring What Matters

And that brings me to the second question: How do we measure being the best? We also measure whether our products — our brands — are better than our competitors. We rank and rate everything — consumer satisfaction, quality, value, awareness, trial, distribution, shelf space, cost and of course market share.

Nobody does it the way Procter & Gamble does it.

Why this obsession with measurement?

So we can find whether we're ahead — or, who's ahead of us, or who is gaining on us and why.

We measure the things that count — the things that add up to market leadership.

Now, these characteristics don't make us unique. Most companies want to be the best. Many rely on measures. But few have the discipline — the rigorous focus on fundamentals — to stay the best. It's our discipline that makes us unique — discipline enables us to achieve market leadership and to sustain it — not just for a quarter or a year but for generations.

Staying Focused on Leadership

Tide has been the number one selling detergent in the U.S. for 45 years. Crest has been the market leader for 32 years. Ariel has been number one in many countries for years. More recently, Always and Pantene have become number one in most of the world. Of all the factors that contribute to Procter & Gamble's success, the sustained pursuit of competitive advantage is the one that ties all the others together — competitive advantage in everything that counts.

And it goes beyond the business itself. Procter & Gamble people not only try to be the best at making and selling soap and paper. We try to be the best at recruiting — at developing our people, at protecting the environment, at supporting the communities in which we work and live. In other words, we strive to be the best at all the things that matter — all the things that contribute to the excellence of our Company.

Even when the Company loses its market leadership — and it happens — we don't give up. We try to figure it out, we try to get it back. It took more than 20 years to reestablish Comet Cleanser as the market leader in the United States, but we persevered — and it's number one again today.

Pringles struggled even longer — nearly 25 years. But the Company persevered until we got the product right, the cost and pricing right and the advertising right. And today, though Pringles is not yet number one in its market, it is a fast-growing $500 million business that's closing in on becoming the global market leader.

This perseverance is another unique Procter & Gamble trait. Our perseverance, coupled with our operating discipline, gives us enormous strength. We must never lose it. These competitive traits, like our core values, are an essential part of our Company culture.

Let's take a closer look at what this competitive edge means to us.

Gaining an Edge Over Competition

There are three core areas in which P&G concentrates on achieving competitive advantage — our products, our work processes and our people.

Our Products

First, product. I don't think there is another company in the world that places so much importance on product superiority. Consistently, the Company's periods of greatest business progress are closely aligned with products that have enjoyed performance advantages over their competition.

It started with Ivory in 1879 — milder than other soaps and a great value. Then came Crisco in 1911 — the first all-vegetable shortening. It outperformed all other cooking fats and literally changed the way America cooked.

Tide — the 1946 washday miracle outcleaned everything else in the market, and Crest in 1955, provided families with a level of cavity protection that had not existed before and that no other brand could offer.

Pampers kept babies drier than cloth and changed diapering habits forever. Ariel in Europe and Latin America cleaned stains that other detergents couldn't budge.

Again and again, Procter & Gamble has set new performance standards with breakthrough technologies. Each product is not only a step change in performance and convenience, but also a major milestone in the Company's history of growth.

Today, with more than 100 established brands, much of the focus has shifted to bringing invention to our existing categories. This is essential as some of these categories are now multi-billion-dollar businesses for us.

Over the last five years, for example, the Company has literally reinvented the Laundry detergent category, first with ultra compact granules, then with ultra liquids and more recently with our Color Guard technology. Right now in Europe, the Company is introducing Ariel Futur, another breakthrough product that sets a new higher standard of cleaning clothes.

This ongoing pursuit of competitive product advantage in the Laundry category has brought the Company to global market leadership, and one of our oldest categories is still one of our fastest growing. Over the last three years, the Company's total Laundry volume worldwide has grown by 14%, adding about two share points to our global share.

Product edge has also grown our Hair Care business. Our 2-in1 shampoo and conditioner technology was a revolutionary innovation that changed this category. It turned Pert Plus and Pantene into market leaders. It is now building our Vidal Sassoon business around the world. Product edge made Procter & Gamble the biggest hair care company in the world.

Innovation has been building virtually every one of our businesses. In each instance, we've achieved an edge over competition because our innovations have met important consumer needs that lead to preference for our brands.

Our Work Processes

We also gain competitive advantage in the way we work. We believe in that. We have always pioneered new approaches. We have continually challenged ourselves to find a better way to get the job done — better than our competitors.

When a Credit Manager implements a new process to improve the payment record of a major account — and, as a result, reduces days outstanding — that moves us toward gaining competitive advantage in cash flow.

Over the last three years, through efforts just like this, we've reduced working capital by over $500 million — to just $200 million or 0.7% of sales — and increased cash flow to a record $3.6 billion. This gives us a stronger credit rating than most of our competitors — a stronger cash position to fund business growth.

Another example comes from the Far East, where our Sales and MSD organizations have turned our distributor network into a powerful source of competitive advantage.

Our Far East distributors cover more than 800,000 outlets. Until recently, they managed virtually all of their operations manually. But we have transformed the way they work with a proprietary Distributor Business System that automates every aspect of their business, from orders to shipping to billing and payments.

This system is building our distributors' businesses — but it's also giving P&G a growing edge over competition. Right Goods, our second largest distributor in the Philippines, has increased volume over 50%, increased service levels to their stores to 95%, and reduced total inventory by 47% — all since converting to our new system.

What has this meant to P&G? A year ago, we had 83% distribution on our laundry brands in the Philippines — dead even with Unilever. Today, Unilever is still at 83%, but we're at 95% and growing.

In addition, we've cut receivables from 14 days to just six. That puts us in a much stronger position to fund growth opportunities than our main competitor: competitive advantage.

Product Supply gives us one of the best examples of all — Operation Stealth, a worldwide program to hold our average Total Delivered Cost per case flat for four years. Global materials sourcing is one key to achieving this. Improving manufacturing reliability at our plants is another.

Reliability is the percentage of time our lines produce good product and are not shut down for changeovers, cleanouts, maintenance, repairs and rework.

In 1991, when Operation Stealth began, P&G plants worldwide averaged only 63% reliability. The flat TDC target required us to get to 85% by 1994/95.

We hit that 85% goal in nearly all of our plants a year ahead of schedule. In fiscal 1993/94, Product Supply produced 1.3 billion cases of product for a unit cost 7% below the worldwide average three years ago. The savings? $1.3 billion after tax. It enabled us to reduce pricing in many categories and deliver better value than our competitors. That's real competitive advantage.

There are many other examples. Virtually every work process in our Company can deliver competitive advantage, and every P&G employee — every one of us — has a role to play in doing it.

Our People

That leads me to our third source of competitive advantage — our people. There is no other aspect of our business where we place as much importance on being the best.

We know the people we hire are in the top 5% of all we interview. Few companies can afford to be that selective. We can, because good people want to work for other good people.
We also work hard to grow our people, to help them develop

through personal training that begins the day they are hired and continues throughout their career. And, we keep expanding and updating our training methods.

P&G College is a recent example of this. And, by the way — the new functional colleges will be up and running in January.

Virtually all of our training has the objective of perpetuating P&G's values, principles and approaches to the business.

We hire the best. We give them tools and training to become even better. And then we dedicate ourselves to giving every individual in the Company a chance to grow and succeed.

That's why we were so very proud to receive the 1994 Opportunity 2000 award from the U.S. Department of Labor. This award, which is given each year to a single American company, recognizes the efforts of men and women throughout our organization to promote and advance all employees — regardless of gender or race or other differences.

This is where we gain our greatest competitive advantage. At every level of the business, we know we have the best people in the job.

One of the remarkable things about P&G people is the way they think about their jobs and their competitors. I can walk into any P&G factory, ask our people what they're doing that gives them an advantage over Unilever, and they can tell me in a minute. And they will. They're oriented to think that way. I can ask a sales manager, "What do you do better than Colgate? And where does Colgate have an advantage over you?" And he or she will tell me that, too.

Perpetuating Our Strengths

This consistency in the quality of our people, this discipline in the way we work, this continual drive to gain a competitive edge doesn't happen by accident. It's quite deliberate, and all of our policies are designed to perpetuate it — but none is more important than promotion from within.

It makes sense for a company that wants to be the best and wants to sustain its competitive advantage to promote from within. Why is that?

Is it to encourage lifetime employment? Yes, but it's more than that.

Is it a way to hang onto good people because they know their future advancement opportunities won't be taken by outsiders? Yes. It is that, too.

But the most important reason we promote from within is that people who have grown up in our culture will work to preserve it and pass it on. That's the one most effective way to perpetuate our Company's values, our discipline and our commitment to competitive advantage.

It's the way we ensure P&G's consistent success. It's what makes Procter & Gamble a very tough competitor.

Wanting to Win – Always

That brings me to a final observation. When I look back over the 41 years I've been with this Company, I'm amazed not so much by what's changed as I am by what has not changed.

At every level of my career, the people I worked for cared as much about my progress as I did. Throughout the organization, that's still true.

I have a real sense of pride in being a Procter & Gamble employee. P&G people want to work with other people who are fair, honest and ethical. That commonality of personal standards gives the Company its character. We are unique in that respect. P&G people want to be leaders. They want to be part of an organization that itself is a leader. They want to accept the responsibility of leadership.

P&G people want to be winners. Everyone likes to win, but P&G people want to win at everything, all the time. That's good because it inspires teamwork and fierceness in the pursuit of competitive advantage.

And, P&G people are good human beings. In fact, I'll bet there is more genuine friendship among P&G people throughout the world than in any company anywhere.

From the day I started, I knew that Procter & Gamble was the kind of company I wanted to work for - where I wanted to spend my career. I've never felt differently, and I know most of you feel the same.

That commitment from P&G people is what has kept this Company successful and will always keep this Company successful — for at least another 157 years.

Keep well, travel safely and God bless you all.

The Obligation of Leadership

January 14, 1995

Mr. Artzt delivered this speech in Atlanta, Georgia, upon accepting the 1995 Martin Luther King Jr. Salute to Greatness Award.

It's overwhelming to receive an award like this ... to stand alongside so many of you — the King family, the Evers family, Dr. Height — people who have given so much and have paid so dearly for the cause of civil rights in this country.

I can't compare my contributions to yours, but I share your conviction. And though I can never fully understand the pain of racism, I have seen the gain that can be achieved from true diversity in the workplace. And I deeply believe that as long as our society permits racism to limit the growth and contribution of talented people, we'll achieve only a fraction of our potential ... as individuals, as organizations, as a nation.

Racism touches every aspect of our lives. It begins in our homes, where children hear things — and develop the fear and false sense of superiority that produce racist behavior in adults. That's why I believe so strongly that we must stop racism early — before it takes root — when people are very young.

It's why P&G has supported programs like the Children's Campaign, which is led by the Leadership Conference Education Fund. This program, which Mrs. King and I co-chair, is reaching children through advertising, classroom videotapes and materials for parents, like the book on your tables — *Talking to Our Children About Prejudice, Racism and Diversity*. We have an obligation to teach our children these lessons.

But we also have an obligation to the men and women who are being affected today by racism.

Five years ago, I was convinced that racism in the workplace was a structural problem — a problem that could be fixed like any other business challenge, with good strategies and clear account-ability for success.

I've learned since then that structural solutions aren't enough. They're important — we're making progress at advancing women and minorities, and we've pretty much eliminated the most obvious blatant forms of racism in our organization, because we've made it clear that overt racist behavior simply won't be tolerated.

But we've had much less success at eliminating the more subtle racism that lurks just under the surface — the kind that Marian Anderson described perfectly when she said, "It's like hair across your cheek. You can't see it, you can't find it with your fingers, but you keep brushing at it, because the feel of it is irritating."

That kind of racism is as debilitating a force today as the ugly brutality of Albany and Birmingham and Selma a generation ago.

When I was here two years ago, I tried to describe my perception of this subtle, beneath-the-surface racism, and I think those words are just as valid today:

I've come to realize that the most subtle forms of racism are sometimes the most destructive, especially in the workplace. Young Black managers I've talked with refer to it as the "pain threshold" — the added burden that results from having one's opinions discount-ed, from failing to receive deserved credit or recognition, or having to work to a different standard than one's peers and seldom receiv-ing the benefit of the doubt in close-call situations. Subtle, debilitat-ing, largely unrecognized racism. We have to deal with this.

But dealing with this kind of racism is harder because it rarely shows its face. Nevertheless, as long as we find its tracks in our companies and in society at large, we must continue to fight it in every way we can.

One way we've done that at P&G is to conduct cultural audits that help us unmask even the most subtle forms of racism within our own organization. These audits, which have been conducted by objective outsiders like Roosevelt Thomas, are invaluable tools because they help us identify aspects of our culture that can disguise and even perpetuate racist behavior. And they help us develop concrete action plans so we can address these issues head-on — and we have.

But I think the most important thing we do — the most important thing any of us can do — is to provide strong personal leadership at every level and especially from the top. To really make a lasting difference, senior managers like me have to roll up our sleeves and get involved in the process.

It's not enough to set numerical targets and challenge the organization to meet them. Instead, the most senior managers in the Company need to know their most promising minority managers — not as statistics, but as individuals. If we want to make change happen, it's our responsibility to find out why those employees are not being advanced, and to personally ensure that they get the development, the coaching and the opportunities they need to move up in the organization.

Without that kind of hands-on involvement by senior management, progress will always come slowly, if at all. But with it, we can create a management culture that will cascade from the top through every level of the organization.

I believe as deeply as I can that those of us who lead must set

strong personal examples — not by merely encouraging diversity
... but by practicing it. Visibly. In our own lives.

That's the real obligation of leadership, and it's an obligation that
I pledge to fulfill as I accept this award.

Thank you.

Edwin Lewis Artzt

Born April 15, 1930 in New York, New York, Edwin Lewis Artzt graduated from the University of Oregon in 1951 and joined Procter & Gamble in December 1953. This is the record of positions held during his Procter & Gamble career:

1953	Sales Training
1954	Assistant Brand Manager
1955	Brand Manager
1958	Associate Brand Promotion Manager
1960	Brand Promotion Manager
	Manager of Copy
1962	Brand Promotion Manager
1965	Manager, Advertising Department, Paper Products Division
1968	Manager, Food Products Division
1969	Vice President, Food Products Division
1970	Vice President, Acting Manager, Coffee Division
	Vice President, Group Executive, U.S.
1972	Member, Board of Directors (1972–1975)
1975	Group Vice President, European Operations
1980	Executive Vice President, International Operations
	Member, Board of Directors
1984	Vice Chairman of the Board and President, Procter & Gamble International
1990	Chairman of the Board and Chief Executive
1995	Chairman of the Executive Committee of the Board of Directors

Acknowledgements

The creation of this bookhas depended on and benefited from the contributions of many people.

First and foremost, of course, has been Ed Artzt himself. He dedicated many hours over the course of multiple meetings and phone calls to define the scope and content of this book and to record his memories and identify the principles flowing from them. Ed spent many more hours editing the transcripts from the interviews and, beyond that, supplementing them through extensive personal research and additional recollections to highlight additional lessons.

Ed's remarkable memory, his sense of what is important and what is not, and his ability to express his memories and learnings in vivid language will make this book of striking relevance to leaders today.

I'm grateful to P&G's Shane Meeker and Greg McCoy, who were instrumental in both recording these interviews and transcribing them and providing photographs and additional material for the book.

Rob Garver, an author and journalist, also participated in the interviews in the process of doing research for a recently published story of John Smale in which Ed Artzt plays a major role.*

We benefited from Cathy Seckman's editorial skills as well as her knowledge of Procter & Gamble as she created the Index for the book.

I am grateful to my assistant, Sue Hermanns, who helped me as she does in all things, in supporting the production of this book.

I want to especially thank the Hyperquake team, a valued and long-term partner of Procter & Gamble's. They stepped forward asking to undertake the design of this book free of cost. The Hyperquake team of Ryan Bedinghaus, Dan Barczak, Tobias Brauer, Scott Dierna and Paige Gutter have devoted countless hours to the design of this book, with all its production elements. They have done so with excellence and care and produced a quality result. We will be forever grateful to them.

John Pepper
Former CEO and Chairman,
Procter & Gamble

*Here Forever: The Timeless Impact of John Smale on P&G, G.M. and the Purpose and Practice of Business.

Index